Student Course Guide for

U.S. History since 1877

Second Edition

KENNETH G. ALFERS, Ph.D.
Dallas County Community College District

DALLAS TeleLearning
Dallas County Community College District
R. Jan LeCroy Center for Educational Telecommunications

BEDFORD / ST. MARTIN'S
Boston • New York

I would like to dedicate this work to Molly, Andrew, Andrea, Aidan, Amalia, Michael, and Isabelle and to all students of history. Special thanks and recognition are due to some special people who greatly enhanced the quality of this course. For two consecutive history telecourse productions, I have worked closely with an exemplary team of dedicated educators. The brilliance and talent of Julia Dyer, producer/director, is most obvious in the twenty-six video programs that give this course its exceptional and unique quality. Julia also wrote the background sketches of our featured families and the "fiction and film" recommendations found in this guide. Working with Julia has been a highlight of my career. Janice Christophel, instructional designer, constantly kept my focus on student learning throughout the two-year production process. She always provided her thoughtful guidance with cordiality and grace. Craig Mayes, director of production, is an exceptional administrator. His encouragement and steady hand always steered us toward the best path. Angie Meyer, production manager and visual image coordinator, lightened our load by applying her superb skills to a multitude of tasks and sharing with us her wit and infectious good spirit.

Mica Marley, production coordinator, was particularly adept at convincing our array of experts to be interviewed and then arranging the intricate details to make that happen. Evelyn J. Wong, telecommunications information specialist, remains a master of the art and technology needed to pull together electronic files from all directions and make this student course guide clear and understandable. Russell Blair, videographer, and Marcia Henke, sound recordist, not only enhanced the videos, but also helped make our production trips enjoyable learning experiences. My colleagues on the national and local advisory committees have my gratitude for their constructive comments throughout the entire process.

Finally, I would like to thank all the members of the staff of the R. Jan LeCroy Center for Educational Telecommunications. This was my fourth stint at doing a project like this, and the help and support of everyone made it another pleasant and rewarding experience.

R. Jan LeCroy Center for Educational Telecommunications

Provost:	Pamela K. Quinn
Vice President of Instruction:	Jim Picquet
History Content Specialist:	Kenneth G. Alfers, Ph.D.
Research Assistant:	Darise Error, Ph.D.
Project Director:	Craig Mayes
Producer/Director:	Julia Dyer
Instructional Designer:	Janice Christophel
Director of Product Design:	Suzanne Dunn, Ph.D.
Production Coordinator:	Mica Marley
Telecommunications Information Specialist:	Evelyn J. Wong

Student Course Guide ISBN (10): 0-312-47004-5: ISBN (13): 978-0-312-47004-3
Copyright © 2009 by Dallas County Community College District.

All rights reserved. No part of this work may be reproduced, transmitted, stored, or used in any form or by any means graphic, electronic, or mechanical, including but not limited to photocopying, recording, scanning, digitizing, taping, Web distribution, information networks, or information storage and retrieval systems, without the prior written permission of the Dallas County Community College District.

Requests for permission to make copies of any part of the work should be mailed to:
Dallas TeleLearning
9596 Walnut Street
Dallas, Texas 75243

BEDFORD / ST. MARTIN'S
75 Arlington Street
Boston, MA 02116

Printed in the United States of America
10 9 8 7 6 5 4 3

Contents

To the Student v
Course Organization vii
Course Guidelines ix
Featured Families xi

UNIT I: INDUSTRIALIZING AMERICA, 1877–1900—"RAGS TO RICHES?"
1. The Gilded Age 3
2. The American West 11
3. Moving to the City 19
4. A Dream Deferred 27
5. Labor's Struggle 35
6. The Populist Challenge 43
7. The Question of Empire 51
   Unit I: Fiction and Film 59

UNIT II: MODERNIZING AMERICA, 1900–1945—"FREEDOM FROM FEAR?"
8. The Progressive Paradox 63
9. A War to End All Wars 71
10. Modern Times 79
11. The Great Depression 87
12. A New Deal 93
13. Road to War 101
14. World at War 109
    Unit II: Fiction and Film 117

UNIT III: REDEFINING AMERICA, 1945–1976—"THE NEW FRONTIERS?"
15. Cold War 121
16. Pursuit of Happiness 129
17. All God's Children 137
18. Times Are A-Changin' 145
19. The Vietnam Dilemma 153
20. The Decline of Liberalism 161
    Unit III: Fiction and Film 169

UNIT IV: RESHAPING AMERICA, 1976–PRESENT—"STILL THE PROMISED LAND?"
21. Conservative Resurgence 173
22. A New Economy 181
23. Life in the Fast Lane 187
24. A Different World 193
25. Globalizing America 201
26. A More Perfect Union 209
    Unit IV: Fiction and Film 217

To the Student

Dear Student:

How many times have you thought about how and why America has become what it is today? Too often in our fast-paced information age, we seem to be overwhelmed with the needs of the present. Those of us in the production of this distance learning course, *Transforming America,* have endeavored to create a comprehensive course of study that challenges you to take the time to think about America and what it means. I urge you to make the most of this opportunity to broaden your knowledge and to reflect upon the past, the present, and the connection between the two.

I have been teaching American history at the college level for more than thirty-five years. During the 2003-2004 and 2004-2005 academic years, I concentrated totally on preparing materials for this telecourse. Friends, colleagues, and former students sometimes smile and question why I devoted so much time to the creation of a new history course. After all, what changes in history? Indeed, that is part of my fascination with the discipline of studying the past, for there is always more to learn. For example, I hope you will be as intrigued as I was by the remarks of the seventy nationally recognized historical experts whom we interviewed for *Transforming America.* Their insights make this course truly unique.

Transforming America surveys U.S. history since 1877 in twenty-six lessons. The textbook and the videos provide you with the content for this distance learning course. The videos use location footage and visual images to remind us that we encounter the past in our daily lives and contemporary communities. Included in the expert historical analysis of important topics in U.S. history found in the videos is an examination of the themes of American identity, freedom, and equality. Also, you will hear from members of our "featured families," whose stories represent the rich diversity of the American experience. Ask yourself where you and your family history fit into this picture.

In summary, I want you to think about the American people, past and present, and to consider our relationships with the rest of the world. Our personal lives, our nation, and our world demand that we analyze, evaluate, and make reasoned judgments about people, leaders, positions, and issues. Our future depends on the prudent application of our knowledge. Through this course of study, it is my hope and expectation that you will gain greater awareness and understanding of America. I also hope that you will come to appreciate your opportunities to create history and help transform America's future.

—Kenneth G. Alfers, Ph.D.

About the Author

Dr. Kenneth G. Alfers is a teacher, writer, and historian. He received the Dallas County Community College District's Outstanding Teacher Award in 1983. In 2005, he was named a Piper Professor for the state of Texas and received the Lifetime Achievement Award for Distance Learning from the Instructional Technology Council. He was the content specialist for *America: The Second Century*, *America in Perspective*, and *Shaping America*, distance learning courses used around the country since 1980. He received his B.A. and M.A. degrees from Creighton University and his M.Ph. and Ph.D. degrees from The George Washington University.

A Final Note

With careful and thoughtful application of your time and energy to the material presented in this course, you should have a rewarding experience in the broadest sense of that term. I, along with other members of the production team, have put forth our best efforts to create a quality course. However, my experience teaches me that any course can be improved, so I encourage you to share any ideas about it with me. Please send your comments to Kenneth G. Alfers, R. Jan LeCroy Center for Educational Telecommunications, 9596 Walnut Street, Dallas, TX 75243-2112.

Course Organization

Transforming America is designed as a comprehensive learning package consisting of four elements: student course guide, textbook, video programs, and interactive activities.

STUDENT COURSE GUIDE

The guide for this course is:

    Alfers, Kenneth G. *Student Course Guide for Transforming America*. 2nd ed., Boston: Bedford/St. Martin's, 2009. ISBN (10): 0-312-47004-5; ISBN (13): 978-0-312-47004-3

This student course guide acts as your daily instructor. Each lesson gives you an Overview, Lesson Assignment, Learning Objectives, Lesson Focus Points, Historical Experts Interviewed, Featured Family Members Interviewed, a Practice Test with an Answer Key, Enrichment Ideas, and Suggested Readings. If you follow the student course guide closely and study each lesson carefully, you should successfully meet all of the requirements for this course.

TEXTBOOK

In addition to the student course guide, the textbook required for this course is:

    Roark, James L., Michael P. Johnson, Patricia Cline Cohen, Sarah Stage, Alan Lawson, and Susan M. Hartmann. *The American Promise: A History of the United States, Volume II: From 1865*. 4th ed. Boston: Bedford/St. Martin's, 2009. ISBN (10): 0-312-45293-4; ISBN (13): 978-0-312-45293-3

VIDEO PROGRAMS

The video program series for this course is:

    Transforming America

Each video program is correlated with the student course guide and the reading assignment for that lesson. Be sure to read the Lesson Focus Points in the student course guide before you watch the program. The video programs are presented in a documentary format and are divided into distinct but connected segments. Every video brings analysis and perspective to the issues being discussed. Watch them closely.

    If the video programs are broadcast more than once in your area, or if video tapes, CDs, DVDs, and streaming are available at your college, you might find it helpful to watch the video programs more than once for review. Also, you may record the programs for review or viewing at a convenient time. Since examination questions will be taken from the video programs as well as from the reading, careful attention to both is vital to your success.

INTERACTIVE COURSE

Self-graded interactive exercises, pre- and post-self-assessments, and case-based, problem-solving scenarios are available to students whose institutions have opted to offer these. These activities are useful for reinforcement and review of lesson content and learning objectives. The interactive activities are offered in two formats: CD-ROM/DVD-ROM, and Internet. Ask your instructor how to access these activities if they are listed in your syllabus as a course requirement.

PUBLISHER'S WEBSITE

The publisher's website is listed at the end of each chapter and at other places in the text. Use it if you desire online review of the material in the text.

Course Guidelines

Follow these guidelines as you study the material presented in each lesson:

1. OVERVIEW:
   Read the Overview for an introduction to the lesson material.

2. LESSON ASSIGNMENT:
   Review the Lesson Assignments in order to schedule your time appropriately. Pay careful attention, as the titles and numbers of the textbook chapters are different from the student course guide lessons and the video programs.

3. LEARNING OBJECTIVES:
   The Learning Objectives in the student course guide tell you what you are expected to learn in each lesson. The material assigned in each lesson is aligned with these objectives and will enable you to achieve them.

4. LESSON FOCUS POINTS:
   The Lesson Focus Points are designed to help you get the most benefit from the resources selected for each lesson. To maximize your learning experience:
   - Scan the focus point questions.
   - Read the material assigned.
   - View the video.
   - Write brief answers to or make notes on the focus point questions. (References in parentheses following each question can be used to locate information in the text and video that relates to each question.)

5. HISTORICAL EXPERTS INTERVIEWED:
   These individuals are acknowledged for their valuable contributions to this course. The titles and locations were accurate when the video programs were produced, but may have changed since the original taping.

6. FEATURED FAMILY MEMBERS INTERVIEWED:
   These individuals are acknowledged for sharing their stories and personalizing the materials presented in this course.

7. PRACTICE TEST:
   Complete the Practice Test to help you evaluate your understanding of the lesson.

8. ANSWER KEY:
   Use the Answer Key at the end of the lesson to check your answers or to locate material related to each question of the Practice Test.

9. ENRICHMENT IDEAS:
   These activities are not required unless your instructor assigns them. They are offered as suggestions to help you learn more about the material presented in this lesson.

10. SUGGESTED READINGS/RESOURCES:
    These reading materials are not required but are offered as suggestions if you wish to examine other books and resources related to the material presented in this lesson.

11. FICTION AND FILM:
    At the end of each unit, selected novels and films are recommended for further enrichment.

12. ADDITIONAL REVIEW:
    The publisher's website for the text is listed throughout each chapter in the text. Use the website if you desire additional review of and/or information about material presented in the text. Also, at the end of each chapter in the text, you will find helpful review steps. Follow these steps to strengthen your understanding of the material in that chapter.

Featured Families

The history we study in school is generally a history of public life. But great or small, all of us create history. Every family adds to the story, enriching the narrative and expanding what it means to be an American.

In *Transforming America*, we explore the histories of eight American families – from the wealthiest and most privileged, to the poorest and most humble. Although they come from widely divergent backgrounds, these families all have one thing in common – somewhere along the way some family member made the decision to dig into the past and uncover the stories that bring the family's legacy to life. In the video programs you will find their trials and triumphs woven into the broader narrative, highlighting the sometimes very personal ways in which the course of history impacted their lives—or their lives impacted the course of history.

The very down-to-earth **Bill Cecil, Jr.** (formally known as Wm. A. Vanderbilt Cecil, Jr.) shares the stories of one of the great industrialist families of the late nineteenth century. A direct descendant of Cornelius Vanderbilt, "The Commodore," Bill describes how his notorious ancestor built the world's greatest fortune; and how Cornelius' grandson, George Vanderbilt, used his share to build the Biltmore, a stunning chateau and working farm in western North Carolina. Today, Bill Cecil and his family still live on the Biltmore Estate, which they operate as a tourist attraction, vineyard, and vacation getaway. Also contributing to the story is Arthur Vanderbilt, a descendant of the Commodore's uncle. He is the author of *Fortune's Children*, a book detailing the history of the Vanderbilt family. (Lessons 1, 4, 8, 19, 21, 22, 24, 25, 26)

Charlene McAden, has spent decades researching and recording the history of the **Lafferty** clan, a family of farmers who moved west to claim a homestead in the Oklahoma Land Rush of 1889. Charlene's great-grandfather, Enoch Lafferty, a Civil War veteran, struggled to make a living on the windswept prairie with his wife, four sons, and a daughter. Eventually, during the Great Depression, Charlene's grandfather was forced to sell the family farm and move into town to raise his eleven children. Charlene herself raised three children during the 1960s, an era that offered them a much wider range of opportunities than she had experienced in her own youth. Her oldest daughter, **Sherrie Tarpley**, weighs in on the significance of coming of age during the women's movement and how that affected her life and that of her daughter. (Lessons 2, 6, 11, 13, 16, 18, 20, 23, 25, 26)

In his book *Singing for a Spirit*, **Vine Deloria, Jr.**, traces his family's history back to a French fur trader, Francois Deloria, who married into a band of Yanktonais Sioux in the late eighteenth century. A hundred years later Vine's great-grandfather Saswe, a Sioux medicine man, encouraged his son to embrace Christianity. The young Tipi Sapa was eventually ordained as the celebrated Episcopal priest Philip Deloria. Philip's son, Vine Deloria, Sr., followed in his father's footsteps to the priesthood. Vine, Jr., however, broke the tradition and went on to become a leading figure in American Indian activism and scholarship. Together with his son, Philip Deloria, Vine shares the story of this family's fascinating journey through the twentieth century. (Lessons 2, 11, 12, 13, 18, 20, 22, 23, 26)

As **Edward Archuleta** puts it, most immigrant families wanted to come to America. In his family's case, America came to them. Ed is a thirteenth generation New Mexican. His ancestors were among the original Spanish families that settled in Santa Fe in 1598. After the war with Mexico in 1848, the United States annexed the Southwest and the Archuletas became American citizens. Much of their land was taken by Anglo-Americans moving into the new territory, but the family managed to hang on and adapt to the new reality. Eventually they came to love their new country, even as they clung strongly to their Hispanic roots. Ed's stories of his family history reflect a changing cultural identity in a changing world. (Lessons 2, 7, 11, 12, 15, 18, 24, 25, 26)

Harry Dingenthal's parents came to America in the great flow of European immigration during the late nineteenth and early twentieth centuries. Harry's father came over in steerage from Polish Austria. Once in New York, he moved into the Jewish neighborhood where the people of his region had settled and found a bride through the services of a matchmaker. The Dingenthal family lived in the tenements where, as Harry remembers, there was never a scrap of food left on anyone's plate. Harry joined the army in the 1930s and served in Europe in World War II, where he was among the first troops to liberate the Nazi concentration camp at Dachau. Harry's stories of growing up as a first generation American are sometimes funny, sometimes poignant, and always memorable. (Lessons 3, 11, 14, 21, 26)

Until he was fifteen years old, **Bill Neebe** never knew that his grandfather was a celebrated labor leader whose activism was honored throughout the world. Oscar Neebe was a German immigrant who settled in Chicago in the 1880s, where he tried to organize labor unions in order to better the lives of the miserable workers. Falsely arrested, tried and convicted as part of a bombing conspiracy, Oscar and his co-defendants were made examples to put the scare into the organized labor movement. His life sentence was later commuted after a pardon from the governor of Illinois, but the effects of his ordeal continued to reverberate through the family for generations. Bill's stories of his family's life on the political left culminate in the reflections of his son, **Mark Neebe** – who honors his great-grandfather's radical legacy, even as he dons a uniform every day to work in law enforcement in the city of Boston. (Lessons 3, 5, 11, 15, 19, 22, 25, 26)

In her fascinating history of Chinese-American women, *Unbound Feet*, **Judy Yung** includes the story of her own great-grandmother, who was sent to the United States in an arranged marriage in the late nineteenth century. She settled in San Francisco and bore five children, but Leong Shee was never happy in America. In 1904 she returned to China, reversing the usual immigrant trend. But Judy's grandmother, who was born in San Francisco before their return to China, made her way back to America while a young woman in her 20s. Judy's family stories have a way of bucking the trend, whether it's her husband **Eddie Fung's** adventures as a teenage POW or her own journey from a sheltered life in Chinatown to political awakening as a modern Asian-American woman. (Lessons 3, 11, 14, 15, 17, 18, 20, 22, 23, 26)

Dianne Swann-Wright traces her family's history back to the plantation on which her ancestors were enslaved. Her book, *A Way Out of No Way*, follows their journey up and out of the economic and psychological slavery that still lingered long after emancipation. Her father, who could neither read nor write, worked for forty years in a back-breaking industrial job to provide for his children the education that was denied him. Today, Dianne holds a Ph.D. and is the curator of African-American history at Monticello, the historic home of Thomas Jefferson. Perhaps her daughter, high school biology teacher **Ellen Wright**, put it best when she said that her family story is a true American triumph. (Lessons 4, 6, 12, 13, 16, 17, 18, 23, 24, 25, 26)

Unit I

Industrializing America
1877–1900
"Rags to Riches?"

1. The Gilded Age
2. The American West
3. Moving to the City
4. A Dream Deferred
5. Labor's Struggle
6. The Populist Challenge
7. The Question of Empire

THEME

One of the most significant outcomes of the Civil War was the triumph of northern industrial capitalism. During the late nineteenth century, the American people experienced what that meant, as the nation underwent a remarkable transformation. Corporate America, with all of its promises and shortcomings, emerged to become the driving force in shaping an America that was quite different from that of pre-Civil War America but quite familiar to those of us living today.

Increasing numbers of people, including immigrants, moved off the land and went to work in the cities. Americans shared the joys of their daily lives and coped with their hardships. Minorities of all sorts found it particularly difficult to pursue the American Dream of rags-to-riches. Toward the end of the century, frustrations prompted both workers and farmers to challenge the power of the political and economic elites. Meanwhile, by the late 1890s, the industrial nation stretched its influence well beyond American boundaries. The nation and the world would never again be the same.

Lesson 1

The Gilded Age

OVERVIEW

When we asked Professor Richard White what he considered to be a key question about United States history since the Civil War, he replied that it "is how a country so utterly transforms itself." Keep that question is mind as we survey the economic, political, social, and diplomatic transformation of America in this course.

In this first lesson, you will hear many other historians raise questions that help direct our study of "how we got from there to here" and remind us "to remember the very vital presence of the past in contemporary American life." This lesson also introduces you to the themes that recur throughout this course. Think about American identity and what that means. Think about freedom and equality, concepts that have been and continue to be contested in America.

The most remarkable transformation of the country in the late nineteenth century involved the change from a primarily agricultural to an industrial nation. American enterprise expanded to unprecedented levels of concentration and production. New heroes emerged, as the "self-made" businessman replaced the "self-reliant" farmers as the ideal American. The culture celebrated great wealth, but the gilded layer of gold at the top of American society concealed some sordid conditions below the surface. How and why had this happened? What were the costs and benefits of this industrializing economy?

LESSON ASSIGNMENT

Text: Roark, et.al., *The American Promise*
- Chapter 18, "Business and Politics in the Gilded Age," pp. 626–663
- Chapter 19, "The City and Its Workers," p. 671

Video: "The Gilded Age," from the series *Transforming America*

LEARNING OBJECTIVES

This lesson introduces the major questions and themes for the course and examines the causes and consequences of industrialization in the late nineteenth century. Upon completion of this lesson, you should be able to:

1. Explain the status of American identity, freedom, and equality in 1876.

2. Analyze the reasons for large-scale industrialization of the United States in the late nineteenth century.

3. Explain how the business class was supported by the culture of the period.

4. Assess the costs and benefits of the rapid industrialization of the United States.

LESSON FOCUS POINTS

The following questions are designed to help you get the most benefit from the sources selected for this lesson. For reference purposes, the video is divided into five segments: (1) Series Introduction, (2) Unit I Open: "America at the Crossroads," (3) "The Rush of the Express," (4) "Luck and Pluck," and (5) Summary Analysis: "Costs and Benefits."

1. What are the key questions we should be asking about American history since 1877? (video segment 1)

2. What did American identity and/or identities mean in 1876? (video segment 2)

3. What did American freedom mean in 1876? What was the relationship between freedom and equality? (video segment 2)

4. What is the origin of the term, "The Gilded Age?" What did the term mean? Why did it become associated with late nineteenth century America? (text, pp. 626–628)

5. How and why did railroads become America's first big business? What roles did Jay Gould, James J. Hill, and Cornelius Vanderbilt play in developing the railroad industry? (text, pp. 628–632; video segment 3)

6. How did the railroads affect economic development? How were they connected to developments in communications? Why was there some public alarm about the railroad industry and railroad magnates? (text, pp. 628–632; video segment 3)

7. How did agricultural production and natural resources affect industrialization? Why was population growth important in this process? (video segment 3)

8. How and why did Andrew Carnegie become such a success in the steel industry? What was meant by "vertical integration?" (text, pp. 632–634)

9. How and why did John D. Rockefeller become dominant in the oil industry? How did the trust and holding company help him achieve his objectives? Why and how did Ida Tarbell criticize Rockefeller? (text, pp. 634–636, 638–639; video segment 3)

10. How did technology affect industrial growth at this time? What notable inventions came into being? Why were inventors like Thomas Alva Edison considered heroes? (text, pp. 639–640, 642–643)

11. How did financiers like J.P. Morgan facilitate the rise of big business? How powerful was Morgan? (text, pp. 641, 644)

12. How and why did the federal government, including the Supreme Court, help business during this era? What was meant by "laissez-faire" capitalism? Why was this a golden era of corruption? (text, pp. 645–647, 653, 656–660; video segment 3)

13. Why were Horatio Alger's stories so popular in the late nineteenth century? Why did the stories create a myth? What was important about this myth? (text, p. 671; video segment 4)

14. What was the theory of Social Darwinism? How did William Graham Sumner spread this theory? How and why did the theory glorify wealth and curb social reform? (text, pp. 644–647; video segment 4)

15. What did Andrew Carnegie say in "The Gospel of Wealth?" How did Carnegie's advice and actions soften social Darwinism? How much influence did Carnegie's view of money have on other millionaires? (text, pp. 644–647; video segment 4)

16. What does a "consumer culture" mean? How is it expressed in the late nineteenth century? (video segment 4)

17. In summary, why did the United States experience rapid industrialization in the late nineteenth century? How did the culture of the time support wealth and big business? What were the costs and benefits of industrialization? How was America transformed during the Gilded Age? (text, all pages; video segments 2-5)

HISTORICAL EXPERTS INTERVIEWED

Kenneth Alfers, Content Specialist for *Transforming America*, Professor of History, Mountain View College, Dallas, TX

Eric Arneson, Professor of History and African American Studies, University of Illinois, Chicago, IL

Michael Bernstein, Professor of History, University of California, San Diego, CA

Julian Bond, Chairman, NAACP Board of Directors, Washington, DC

Kevin Boyle, Associate Professor, Ohio State University, Columbus, OH

H.W. Brands, Professor of History, University of Texas, Austin, TX

Albert Camarillo, Professor of History, Stanford University, Stanford, CA

Clayborne Carson, Professor of History and Editor of Martin Luther King, Jr. Papers, Stanford University, Stanford, CA

Eric Foner, Professor of History, Columbia University, New York, NY

David Gutierrez, Professor, University of California, San Diego, CA

Steven Hahn, Professor of History, University of Pennsylvania, Philadelphia, PA

Susan Hartmann, Professor of History, Ohio State University, Columbus, OH

Joan Hoff, Research Professor of History, Montana State University, Bozeman, MT

Alice Kessler-Harris, Professor of History, Columbia University, New York, NY

Michael Kazin, Professor of History, Georgetown University, Washington, DC

Pamela W. Laird, Associate Professor, University of Colorado, Denver, CO

David Levering Lewis, Professor of History, New York University, New York, NY

Patricia Limerick, Faculty Director, Center of the American West, University of Colorado, Boulder, CO

—*Continued*

HISTORICAL EXPERTS INTERVIEWED—*Continued*

Julianne Malveaux, Economist and Author, Last Wave Productions, Washington, DC
Michael McGerr, Professor of History, Indiana University, Bloomington, IN
Lisa McGirr, Dunwalke Associate Professor, Harvard University, Cambridge, MA
Bruce Schulman, Professor of History, Boston University, Boston, MA
Sarah Stage, Professor, Arizona State University, West Campus, Phoenix, AZ
Susan Strasser, Professor of History, University of Delaware, Newark, DE
Richard White, Professor of History, Stanford University, Stanford, CA

FEATURED FAMILY MEMBERS INTERVIEWED

Bill Cecil, Jr., Asheville, NC
Arthur Vanderbilt, Roseland, NJ

PRACTICE TEST

The following items will help you evaluate your understanding of this lesson. Use the Answer Key at the end of the lesson to check your answers or to locate material related to this lesson.

Multiple Choice: Choose the letter of the best answer.

1. One of the most important ways that the past affects the present is _____.
   A. shaping decisions we make and options presented to us
   B. proving that America always takes the moral high ground
   C. helping us predict outcomes of future events
   D. assuring us of continued American exceptionalism

2. By 1876, American freedom _____.
   A. had narrowed in its meaning for most Americans
   B. would not be contested in America any more
   C. had been exalted as the key national principle in American life
   D. became a guiding principle of government relations with American Indians

3. When he died in 1892, Jay Gould was described as both "the world's richest man" and "the most hated man in America," an indication that _____.
   A. most Americans were envious of his accomplishments
   B. he symbolized what most troubled the public about the rise of big business
   C. something had gone awry in the calculation of his wealth
   D. the distribution of wealth had become more equitable

4. Railroads were critical to industrial growth for all of the following reasons EXCEPT _____.
   A. spreading settlements across the nation
   B. establishing standards for worker safety
   C. facilitating the expansion of the telegraph
   D. distributing raw materials and finished products

5. Ida M. Tarbell's "History of the Standard Oil Company" in *McClure's Magazine* depicted John D. Rockefeller as _____.
   A. a benevolent businessman who provided cheap kerosene to millions
   B. an inept businessman whose success rested on overworked managers
   C. a success and a model for others hoping to prosper in business
   D. a ruthless and unscrupulous corporate manager

6. The prominent business leaders of the late nineteenth century _____.
   A. thought they were making American business more democratic
   B. despised competition and tried to achieve central control of a business
   C. promised they would give all their money away before they died
   D. believed it was their Christian faith that led to their fabulous success in business

7. The concept of laissez-faire was undermined in the late nineteenth century in part because _____.
   A. the Supreme Court increasingly reinterpreted the Constitution to protect business
   B. many Americans were not quite sure what it was or how it functioned
   C. the president frequently acted to the detriment of big business
   D. Republicans and Democrats in Congress could not agree on its tenets

8. The rags-to-riches myth in American history _____.
   A. supported the creation of welfare programs
   B. diminished the status of the wealthy
   C. served to give people hope
   D. exposed the corruption among the industrial elite

9. All of the following were associated with the consumer culture emerging in the late nineteenth century EXCEPT _____.
   A. more manufactured items were available for purchase
   B. advertising created the desire to want more things
   C. worldly goods were used to measure success
   D. labeling of products being sold to the public

Short Answer: Your answer should specifically address the points indicated in one or two paragraphs.

10. How and why did Cornelius Vanderbilt and his family represent the Gilded Age?

11. How and why did the federal government, including the Supreme Court, aid business in the late nineteenth century?

12. Why was the theory of Social Darwinism popular among the rich? How did this theory affect the poor?

Essay Question: Your response should be several paragraphs long and should elaborate on the points indicated in a manner that expresses understanding of the material.

13. Explain at least five reasons for the rapid industrialization of the United States in the late nineteenth century. How did the culture of the time support wealth and big business? How was America transformed during the Gilded Age? What was the legacy of this era of American history?

ANSWER KEY

Answer	Learning Objectives	Focus Points	References
1. A	LO 1	FP 1	Video segment 1
2. C	LO 1	FP 3	Video segment 2
3. B	LO 2	FP 5	Text, pp. 628–632
4. B	LO 2	FP 6	Text, pp. 628–632; video segment 3
5. D	LO 2	FP 9	Text, pp. 636, 638–639
6. B	LO 2	FP 11	Text, pp. 641, 644
7. A	LO 3	FP 12	Text, pp. 645–647
8. C	LO 3	FP 13	Text, p. 671; video segment 4
9. D	LO 3, 4	FP 16	Video segment 4

10. .... LO 2–4 .... FP 5 .... Text, pp. 628–632; video segment 3
    - What personal qualities did the Commodore possess?
    - How did he take advantage of the opportunities he had?
    - How did he treat his adversaries? What was his attitude toward government?
    - How did he and his family flaunt their wealth?

11. .... LO 2, 3 .... FP 12 .... Text, pp. 645–647, 653, 656–660; video segment 3
    - Consider how subsidies and tariffs helped business.
    - Why was there little regulation? Why were the regulations that existed hardly enforced?
    - How did the Supreme Court protect and enlarge the rights of business?

12. ....LO 3......................FP 14.. Text, pp. 644–647; video segment 4
    - What was the theory of Social Darwinism? How did it flatter the rich?
    - Why did this theory support laissez-faire capitalism?
    - Why are people poor, according to Social Darwinists? What can be done for them?

13. ....LO 2–4..................FP 17.. Text, all pages; video segments 2–5
    - Consider natural resources, population growth/labor, capital, transportation/communications, marketing, technology, management/entrepreneurs, and the role of government.
    - Consider the effects of the Alger myth, Social Darwinism, and consumer culture.
    - What were the big changes that took place in the nation?
    - What were the costs and benefits of industrialization?

ENRICHMENT IDEAS

These activities are not required unless your instructor assigns them. They are offered as suggestions to help you learn more about the material presented in this lesson.

1. Read the "Documenting the American Promise" segment in the text (pp. 638–639) on "Rockefeller and His Critics." In a well-developed essay, thoroughly answer the questions posed in the text.

2. In the "Gospel of Wealth," Andrew Carnegie wrote: "The man who dies thus rich dies disgraced." Write a well-developed essay in which you analyze why Carnegie wrote that passage and what he meant by it. Do you agree with him?

SUGGESTED READINGS/RESOURCES

See the "Bibliography" on pages 660–661 of the text if you wish to examine other books and resources related to the material discussed in this lesson.

Lesson 2

The American West

OVERVIEW

The trans-Mississippi West held a special place in the American imagination for much of the late nineteenth and twentieth centuries. As Professor Patricia Limerick muses in the video for this lesson, at first it may seem strange that "a cultural myth involving single white guys on horses and open spaces" develops as the nation is experiencing industrialization and urbanization. But imagination sometimes helps us escape reality, including the realities of life in the American West in the late nineteenth century.

Historians now stress how connected the West was to Gilded Age America. Railroads were vital in linking the West to other parts of the country. Mining, ranching, and farming became commercial enterprises tied in with national and international markets. As elsewhere, some people profited, and many struggled to survive.

Among those who struggled the most were thousands of American Indians and Mexican Americans who had long been living in the West. Sadly, cultural clashes in the late nineteenth century would result in both groups losing a sense of place. How and why did this happen? More generally, how did the real changes occurring in the West during the Gilded Age transform America?

LESSON ASSIGNMENT

Text: Roark, et. al., *The American Promise*
- Chapter 17, "The Contested West," pp. 590–625

Video: "The American West," from the series *Transforming America*

LEARNING OBJECTIVES

This lesson examines the causes and consequences of the transformations taking place in the American West in the late nineteenth century. Upon completion of this lesson, you should be able to:

1. Describe the economic and social changes occurring in the West during this era and how these changes were connected to the rest of America.

2. Explain why people moved into the West and how they coped with the conditions they faced.

3. Explain how American Indians responded to their plight.

4. Analyze the attempts to assimilate American Indians and to displace Mexican Americans living in the West.

5. Assess the legacy of the transformation of the West.

LESSON FOCUS POINTS

The following questions are designed to help you get the most benefit from the sources selected for this lesson. For reference purposes, the video is divided into five segments: (1) Introduction, (2) "The Promised Land," (3) "Conquest and Survival," (4) "A Sense of Place," and (5) Summary Analysis: "The Western Myth."

1. How and why did mining on the Comstock Lode and other areas in the West reflect the industrialization going on in other parts of the country in the late nineteenth century? (text, pp. 603–608; video segment 2)

2. Why was "hydraulic mining" used in the West? How did it affect mining operations? What effect did this process have on the environment? (text, pp. 604–605)

3. What characterized the operations of territorial government in the West? (text, pp. 608–609)

4. How and why did the federal government and the railroads encourage economic development of the West? Why did people move West? (text, pp. 612–621; video segment 2)

5. How did cattle ranching evolve in the West between 1865 and 1900? Why did barbed wire revolutionize the cattle business? How was ranching similar to other businesses of the era? (text, pp. 615, 618; video segment 2)

6. Who were the "Exodusters?" Why did tenancy, sharecropping, and migrant farm labor become common in the West? (text, pp. 618–619)

7. Why was farming on the Great Plains so difficult? How did farmers cope? (text, pp. 619–621; video segment 2)

8. Why did the number of farms increase during this era? Why did the percentage of the American population who were rural decrease? (text, pp. 619–621)

9. How did mechanization affect farming? Why was farming becoming more commercial? How did the Miller & Lux company illustrate agribusiness? How had the ideal of the self-sufficient yeoman farmer been transformed? (text, pp. 619–621; video segment 2)

10. Who comprised the diverse peoples of the West? What tensions existed among these people? How were these tensions expressed? (text, pp. 609–611)

11. How and why were lives of the American Indians in the West being affected by the socio-economic transformations taking place in that region? What choices did they have in light of the conditions they faced? (text, pp. 591–596; video segment 3)

12. What factors led to the "Indian wars" between the 1860s and 1890? In particular, what brought U.S. troops and American Indians to the Little Bighorn River in June 1876? What happened there? What were the consequences? (text, pp. 593–597, 600; video segment 3)

13. Who was Chief Joseph? How did he express the plight of the American Indians? How did the Apache tribes and Geronimo carry on with resistance? (text, p. 601)

14. Why did Ghost Dancing become popular among Indian tribes in 1889-1890? How was Ghost Dancing connected to the massacre at Wounded Knee in 1890? What happened there? What were the consequences of this massacre? (text, pp. 602–603; video segment 3)

15. Generally, how did Indians view assimilation in the late nineteenth century? Why was Christianity attractive to some Indians? Why did the government subsidize missionaries? (video segment 4)

16. What was the purpose of Indian boarding schools? What happened at these schools? What were the consequences? (text, pp. 591–592; video segment 4)

17. Why was the Dawes Act passed? What were its results? (text, p. 600; video segment 4)

18. How and why did so much land in the West change ownership from Mexican Americans to Anglo Americans during this era? What were the consequences for Mexican Americans of the decline in their land ownership? (text, pp. 609–610; video segment 4)

19. How did Mexican Americans cope with the conditions they faced? How and why did they form a uniquely Mexican American identity? (video segment 4)

20. Why did a western myth emerge out of the developments of the Gilded Age? How and why was that myth passed on to later generations? (text, pp. 621–622; video segments 1, 5)

21. In summary, how and why was the West transformed in the late nineteenth century? How did these changes affect the people who lived in the West? How did the changes in the West transform America? (text, all pages; video segments 1–5)

HISTORICAL EXPERTS INTERVIEWED

Gerard Baker, Superintendent, Mount Rushmore National Memorial, Keystone, SD

Deena Gonzalez, Professor and Chairperson of Chicano Studies, Loyola Marymount University, Los Angeles, CA

Fred Hoxie, Professor of History, University of Illinois, Urbana/Champaign, IL

Patricia Limerick, Faculty Director, Center of the American West, University of Colorado, Boulder, CO

Yolanda Romero, Professor of History, North Lake College, Irving, TX

Richard White, Professor of History, Stanford University, Stanford, CA

FEATURED FAMILY MEMBERS INTERVIEWED

Edward Archuleta, Santa Fe, NM
Vine Deloria, Jr., Golden, CO
Charlene McAden, Blooming Grove, TX

PRACTICE TEST

The following items will help you evaluate your understanding of this lesson. Use the Answer Key at the end of the lesson to check your answers or to locate material related to this lesson.

Multiple Choice: Choose the letter of the best answer.

1. The development of the West between 1870 and 1890 was _____.
    A. separate and unique from that of the rest of the nation
    B. not connected to the growth of large cities
    C. an important part of a nationwide transformation
    D. relatively free from racial and ethnic tensions

2. The wealth produced in the Nevada mining industry primarily _____.
    A. enriched speculators in San Francisco and other cities
    B. remained in the state's rapidly expanding mining towns
    C. was used to fund local education and construction projects
    D. discouraged immigrants from migrating to the region

3. In the three decades after 1870, hundreds of thousands of Americans migrated to the West to _____.
    A. find work in the steel industry
    B. own their own land
    C. serve in territorial government
    D. earn wages in agribusiness

4. All of the following were associated with cattle ranching in the late nineteenth century EXCEPT _____.
    A. shortage of wage laborers
    B. distribution of products by railroads
    C. techniques of mass production
    D. investment of foreign capital

5. Henry Miller and Charles Lux can best be described as _____.
    A. the Andrew Carnegie and John D. Rockefeller of the far West
    B. small ranchers in New Mexico
    C. enlightened benefactors of migrant laborers
    D. adherents to the ideal of the self-sufficient yeoman farmer

6. The buffalo herds on the Great Plains were decimated by _____.
   A. Native Americans who slaughtered the animals for their rituals
   B. U.S. soldiers provisioning western forts
   C. both buffalo hunters hired by the railroads and irresponsible sportsmen
   D. Chinese and Irish work gangs who were desperate for food

7. At the Little Bighorn River in Montana in June 1876, Sioux Indians _____.
   A. launched an unprovoked attack on settlers
   B. defeated federal troops led by George Custer
   C. rejected the terms of the Fort Laramie Treaty
   D. secured their hunting grounds for future generations

8. From the perspective of American Indians in the late nineteenth century, all of the following aspects of assimilation were of interest EXCEPT _____.
   A. adopting Christianity
   B. engaging in farming
   C. learning English
   D. embracing boarding schools

9. Mexican Americans in the West in the late nineteenth century _____.
   A. did not maintain contact with Mexico
   B. controlled territorial politics
   C. refused to exercise citizenship rights
   D. lost title to vast amounts of land

10. The proliferation of dime novels and outfits like William F. Cody's Wild West Company _____.
    A. painted a generally realistic portrait of life in the Old West
    B. spurred legislators to propose laws to clean up corruption in western mining operations
    C. depicted Native Americans as honorable men and women who had been victimized by white greed and encroachment
    D. mythologized and romanticized life in the Old West

Short Answer: Your answer should specifically address the points indicated in one or two paragraphs.

11. Why did Ghost Dancing become popular among American Indians in 1889-1890? Why did it frighten non-Indians?

12. What conditions did Mexican Americans face in the West in the late nineteenth century? How did they cope? What were the consequences of this era of Mexican American history?

13. Briefly describe the western myth. Why was this myth created? What purposes did it serve?

Essay Question: Your response should be several paragraphs long and elaborate on the points indicated in a manner that expresses understanding of the material.

14. How and why was the West transformed in the late nineteenth century? How did these changes affect the people living in the West? How did the changes in the West transform America?

ANSWER KEY

	Answer	Learning Objectives	Focus Points	References
1.	C	LO 1	FP 1, 4, 5, 9	Text, pp. 603–608, 612–621; video segment 2
2.	A	LO 1	FP 1	Text, pp. 603–608
3.	B	LO 2	FP 4	Text, pp. 612–621; video segment 2
4.	A	LO 1	FP 5	Text, pp. 615, 618; video segment 2
5.	A	LO 2	FP 9	Text, pp. 619–621
6.	C	LO 3	FP 11	Text, pp. 591–596; video segment 3
7.	B	LO 3	FP 12	Text, pp. 597, 600; video segment 4
8.	D	LO 4	FP 15	video segment 4
9.	D	LO 4	FP 18	Text, pp. 609–610; video segment 4
10.	D	LO 3	FP 20	Text, pp. 621–622; video segments 1–5

11. .... LO 3 .... FP 14 .... Text, pp. 602–603; video segment 3
    - Consider the plight of American Indians in 1889-1890.
    - What do people tend to do in times of stress? What life did Indians desire?
    - What did non-Indians have at stake?

12. .... LO 4 .... FP 18, 19 .... Text, pp. 609–610; video segment 4
    - What was happening with land ownership in that region?
    - What forms of discrimination existed? What were the opportunities?
    - What types of assistance and/or resistance were available?
    - How did conditions affect status and identity?

13. .... LO 5 .... FP 20 .... Text, pp. 621–622; video segment 1, 5
    - Who were the heroes in this myth? How was the story told?
    - How did the myth allow for escaping reality?
    - What did the myth justify?

14. .... LO 1–5 .... FP 1–21 .... Text, all pages; video segments 1–5
    - Consider the economic, social, and political forces at work.
    - Why were the railroads and the federal government critical?
    - How did mining, ranching, and farming change in the West?
    - How were American Indians, Mexican Americans, and settlers affected?
    - How was the West connected to the rest of the country?
    - What role did the western myth play in American history?

ENRICHMENT IDEAS

These activities are not required unless your instructor assigns them. They are offered as suggestions to help you learn more about the material presented in this lesson.

1. Read the "Documenting the American Promise" segment in the text (pp. 616–617) on "Young Women Homesteaders and the Promise of the West." In a well-developed essay, answer the questions posed in the text.

2. You are a man or woman settler, an American Indian, or Mexican American living in the West in the 1880s and 1890s. Prepare a letter or a speech in which you explain your plight and what you are going to do about it.

SUGGESTED READINGS/RESOURCES

See the "Bibliography" on pages 622–623 of the text if you wish to examine other books and resources related to the material discussed in this lesson.

Lesson 3

Moving to the City

OVERVIEW

Of all the changes occurring during the rapid industrialization of America during the late nineteenth century, the growth of cities was perhaps the most dramatic. Millions of people moved to cities like New York, Chicago, and San Francisco, seeking employment and other opportunities. Ironically, most of these "huddled masses" came from rural areas, as advances in agricultural production reduced the relative need for as many farmers as in the past.

Getting to the city became easier, but once there, life could be hard. Immigrants had to adapt to new surroundings and could face hostility from nativists who tried to exclude them from being an "American." Crowded close to their work, the new arrivals often lived in deplorable conditions. City services seldom kept up with the burgeoning population.

Through it all, people coped as best they could. They changed urban America even as they were being changed by it. A new national culture was emerging from the blending taking place in America's cities. Who are these people? What are their stories? What can we learn from their experiences?

LESSON ASSIGNMENT

Text: Roark, et. al., *The American Promise*
- Chapter 19, "The City and its Workers," pp. 665–677, 688–703

Video: "Moving to the City," from the series *Transforming America*

LEARNING OBJECTIVES

This lesson examines the causes and consequences of rapid urbanization of the United States in the late nineteenth century. Upon completion of this lesson, you should be able to:

1. Explain why the population of American cities grew so rapidly during this era.

2. Explain the causes and consequences of the massive immigration of this time.

3. Assess the social and political effects of this urbanization process.

4. Examine how people coped with urban conditions.

5. Assess how this era of urbanization and immigration transformed America.

LESSON FOCUS POINTS

The following questions are designed to help you get the most benefit from the sources selected for this lesson. For reference purposes, the video is divided into five segments: (1) Introduction, (2) "The Big Apple," (3) "City of Broad Shoulders," (4) "Gold Mountain," and (5) Summary Analysis: "A National Culture."

1. Why was there a global migration from rural areas to cities in the late nineteenth century? (text, pp. 666–672; video segments 1, 2)

2. Who was coming to American cities? Why were they coming? (text, pp. 667–672, 674–675; video segment 2)

3. What distinguishes "old" immigrants from "new" immigrants? What process did immigrants go through at Ellis Island? (text, pp. 668–672; video segment 2)

4. Examine map 19.2 on page 669 of the text. How would you answer the questions posed there? (text, p. 669)

5. How and why did the social geography of the cities change in the late nineteenth century? Where did immigrants tend to live? What occupations did they tend to pursue? (text, pp. 676–677; video segment 2)

6. What was it like to live in the tenements in New York City? How did Jacob Riis expose living conditions there? How did those conditions contrast with the lifestyles of the rich? How did reformers try to change tenement conditions? (text, pp. 676–677; video segment 2)

7. How and why was the cult of domesticity reinforced for middle-class families during the Gilded Age? What was the "separate sphere" for women? Why did domestic servants become more common? (text, pp. 688–689)

8. What characterized mill towns and company towns? What amusements became popular among the middle and working classes? What effects did schools and libraries have on urban life? (text, pp. 689–694)

9. How and why was the urban landscape changing? How did public works projects change the cities? How did landscape architects like Frederick Law Olmsted transform urban life? (text, pp. 691–694)

10. Who were the city "bosses?" How did they get and keep power? Who benefited from bossism? (text, pp. 694–697; video segment 2)

11. Why did Chicago emerge as a major American city in the late nineteenth century? Why did it become known as the "City of Broad Shoulders?" (text, pp. 696–699; video segment 3)

12. How and why were Chicago's slums different from those in New York City? How did the working poor in Chicago cope with the conditions they faced? What functions did saloons serve? (video segment 3)

13. What was important about the World's Columbian Exposition in Chicago in 1893? What did it represent? How did the "White City" contrast with the realities of Chicago? (text, pp. 696–699; video segment 3)

14. Why did Chinese immigrants come to California? Why and how did Chinese American laborers help build railroads during this era? (text, p. 673; video segment 4)

15. What is "nativism?" How were nativists defining "race" in the late nineteenth century? Why was the Chinese Exclusion Act passed in 1882? What was important about this legislation? (text, pp. 672–673, 676; video segment 4)

16. Why and how did many Chinese Americans maintain transnational ties? How was this reflected in Judy Yung's family history? (video segment 4)

17. How was Chinese American identity shaped by developments in the late nineteenth century? (video segment 4)

18. How and why is the Brooklyn Bridge a fitting symbol of the rise of urban America? (text, pp. 664–666; video segment 5)

19. In summary, how and why were cities transformed in the late nineteenth century? How did cities transform America? (text, all pages; video segments 1–5)

HISTORICAL EXPERTS INTERVIEWED

Leonard Dinnerstein, Professor Emeritus, University of Arizona, Tucson, AZ
Perry Duis, Professor of History, University of Illinois at Chicago, Chicago, IL
Sarah Stage, Professor, Arizona State University, West Campus, Phoenix, AZ
Judy Wu, Assistant Professor, Ohio State University, Columbus, OH

FEATURED FAMILY MEMBERS INTERVIEWED

Harry Dingenthal, Garland, TX
Bill Neebe, Wilmette, IL
Judy Yung, Santa Cruz, CA

PRACTICE TEST

The following items will help you evaluate your understanding of this lesson. Use the Answer Key at the end of the Practice Test to check your answers or to locate material related to each question.

Multiple Choice: Choose the letter of the best answer.

1. The astonishing growth in urban population between 1870 and 1900 was largely the product of _____.
   A. annexation of areas surrounding major cities
   B. rising birthrates within the United States
   C. movement of people from other areas of the country and from abroad
   D. failure of agriculture to grow enough food

2. In the late nineteenth century, people moved to American cities because they were seeking all of the following EXCEPT _____.
   A. excitement
   B. jobs
   C. healthy environments
   D. better lives

3. Beginning in the 1880s, "new" immigrants to America typically came from _____.
   A. northern and western Europe
   B. western Europe almost exclusively
   C. southern Europe almost exclusively
   D. eastern and southern Europe

4. Living conditions in late nineteenth century American cities were characterized by _____.
   A. crowded and unsanitary environments
   B. decline in ethnic neighborhoods
   C. integration of people by race and class
   D. lack of community life

5. Throughout much of the nineteenth century, middle-class American women were confined by a cultural ideology that dictated that they _____.
   A. work outside the home to make ends meet
   B. integrate workplace and home as much as possible
   C. make their household a separate sphere
   D. extend their sphere of influence to include charity work

6. Beginning in the 1870s, American men of all classes were united in their passion for _____.
   A. baseball
   B. dance halls
   C. theater
   D. church socials

7. In the post–Civil War era, the city boss _____.
   A. usually was the mayor
   B. provided social services for new residents
   C. seldom controlled construction in the city
   D. was a city councilor who had served at least three consecutive terms

8. Chicago became a major city in the late nineteenth century because it was a _____.
   A. railroad hub
   B. baseball mecca
   C. state capital
   D. refuge for socialists

9. In the video, "Moving to the City," the story of Judy Yung's family in the late nineteenth and early twentieth century illustrates how Chinese Americans _____.
   A. displaced Mexican Americans living in northern California
   B. became successful in the laundry business
   C. formed powerful political coalitions in San Francisco
   D. maintained transnational family ties

10. At the end of the nineteenth century, the Brooklyn Bridge stood as a symbol of _____.
    A. importance of American rivers
    B. decline of immigration to the United States
    C. ascendancy of urban America
    D. frontier spirit in America

Short Answer: Your answer should specifically address the points indicated in one or two paragraphs.

11. How were the experiences of Chinese Americans in the late nineteenth century similar to and different from the experiences of Mexican Americans at that time?

12. Why did nativism flare up in the late nineteenth century? How did nativists try to define Americanism? Who were the targets of their scorn?

13. How did technology transform the urban landscape of America in the late nineteenth century?

Essay Question: Your response should be several paragraphs long and should elaborate on the points indicated in a manner that expresses understanding of the material.

14. How and why were cities transformed in America in the late nineteenth century? How did cities and the people living in them transform America?

ANSWER KEY

	Answer	Learning Objectives	Focus Points	References
1.	C	LO 1	FP 1	Text, pp. 666–672; video segment 2
2.	C	LO 1	FP 2	Text, pp. 667–672, 674–675; video segment 2
3.	D	LO 2	FP 3	Text, pp. 668–672; video segment 2
4.	A	LO 3	FP 6	Text, pp. 676–677; video segment 2
5.	C	LO 4	FP 7	Text, pp. 688–689
6.	A	LO 4	FP 8	Text, pp. 690–691
7.	B	LO 3	FP 10	Text, pp. 694–697; video segment 2
8.	A	LO 1	FP 11	Video segment 3
9.	D	LO 2, 4, 5	FP 16	Video segment 4
10.	C	LO 5	FP 18	Text, pp. 664–666; video segment 5

11. ....LO 2, 5..................FP 14–17......................Text, pp. 672–673, 676; video segment 4
    - Consider their respective standing in American society.
    - How did others view them? How were they treated?
    - How did they cope? How were their identities affected?

12. ....LO 2....................FP 15...............Text, pp. 672–673, 676; video segment 4
    - Why were nativists worried about immigrants at that time?
    - Who did nativists consider to be true Americans?
    - How did they discriminate against "new" immigrants?

13. ....LO 1, 3, 5............FP 9....................... Text, pp. 691–694; video segments 1–5
    - Consider the differences between the pre-industrial and industrial cities.
    - What effect did the use of iron and steel have?
    - How did the elevator, sewer and water systems, and public works affect urban life?

14. ....LO 5....................FP 19....................... Text, all pages; video segments 1–5
    - Consider the internal and global effects of the industrial revolution.
    - Why did so many immigrants come to the cities? Where did they live?
    - How and why did the social geography of cities change?
    - How did technology affect urban life?
    - How did urban governments deal with the changes in cities?
    - How and why did a new national culture emerge? How did cities challenge the American promise?

ENRICHMENT IDEAS

These activities are not required unless your instructor assigns them. They are offered as suggestions to help you learn more about the material presented in this lesson.

1. Imagine yourself to be an immigrant from Europe or Asia in the late nineteenth century. Write a two-page letter to relatives back home in which you describe housing, work, and opportunity in the United States. Would you tell them to join you or not?

2. If any of your relatives were immigrants to the United States in the late nineteenth or early twentieth centuries, investigate their experiences (use oral history, letters, photographs, etc.). Write a two-page report in which you describe their experiences (cite your sources).

3. Read *How the Other Half Lives* by Jacob Riis. Then write a critical analysis of the book in which you describe its main themes and give a personal evaluation of it.

4. Research the histories of Ellis Island and Angel Island as they relate to immigration history. In a well-developed essay, compare and contrast what occurred in these two locations. What goes on at these places today?

5. If you live in a city that changed significantly in the late nineteenth century, research the local history. Submit an essay in which you summarize your findings and comment on how what happened then still affects the city today.

SUGGESTED READINGS/RESOURCES

See the "Bibliography" on pages 700–701 if you wish to examine other books and resources related to the material discussed in this lesson.

Lesson 4

A Dream Deferred

OVERVIEW

As we have seen, coping with changes wrought by the spread of industrial capitalism in the late nineteenth century was difficult for most Americans. In addition, minorities faced their own set of challenges. American Indians and Mexican Americans were often pushed aside as development spread westward. Nativists targeted new immigrants for discrimination, and Chinese laborers were even singled out for exclusion from the country. Meanwhile, African Americans and women of all ethnic groups had to deal with special difficulties in their pursuit of happiness. Promises of freedom were often broken; dreams of equality were often deferred.

The end of the Civil War and the constitutional amendments adopted during Reconstruction seemed to assure a "new birth of freedom" for African Americans. Some were able to enjoy the fruits of their labor. However, the realities of persistent racism, terrorism, economic barriers, and political restrictions shattered the dreams of most. When the Supreme Court (1896) approved "separate but equal" facilities in the Plessy decision, it sanctioned a segregated society that was not equal.

Discrimination aimed at women had no ethnic or racial boundaries, but minority women endured a double dose of it. Women activists of the late nineteenth century were disappointed by the limited reach of the Civil War amendments and pursued gender equity and reforms on a number of fronts. They made some gains, but resistance was strong.

What can we learn from the experience of African Americans and women during this era? What is the legacy of their struggle?

LESSON ASSIGNMENT

Text: Roark, et. al., *The American Promise*
- Chapter 18, "Business and Politics in the Gilded Age," pp. 649–653
- Chapter 19, "The City and Its Workers," pp. 672–677
- Chapter 20, "Dissent, Depression, and War," pp. 704–706, 720–722
- Chapter 21, "Progressivism from the Grass Roots to the White House," pp. 778–782

Video: "A Dream Deferred," from the series *Transforming America*

LEARNING OBJECTIVES

This lesson examines the status of African Americans and women in the late nineteenth century and how those groups responded to their plight. Upon completing this lesson, you should be able to:

1. Explain how and why African Americans faced discrimination in this era.

2. Analyze the responses of African Americans, particularly as expressed by recognized black leaders, to the conditions they faced.

3. Analyze the conditions faced by women at this time and how they were attempting to change the status quo.

4. Assess the legacy of this era of African American and women's history.

LESSON FOCUS POINTS

The following questions are designed to help you get the most benefit from the sources selected for this lesson. For reference purposes, the video is divided into five segments: (1) Introduction, (2) "Strange Fruit," (3) "Hammering at the Truth," (4) "A Very Gendered Thing," and (5) Summary Analysis: "The Legacy of Struggle."

1. How does the poem recited at the beginning of the video express the possibilities existing when a dream is deferred? (video introduction)

2. What was meant by a "New South" in the late nineteenth century? To what extent was the "New South" different from the Old South, particularly for African Americans? (text, pp. 649–651; video segment 2)

3. What economic problems were inherent in sharecropping? (video segment 2)

4. What were Jim Crow laws? What was the significance of the *Plessy v. Ferguson* decision? (text, pp. 779–782; video segment 2)

5. How and why were black voters denied the right to vote in the late nineteenth century? (text, p. 779; video segment 2)

6. How did lynching illustrate the southern horrors facing blacks? What were the long-term effects of the physical and psychological intimidation of blacks by whites? (text, pp. 650–651; video segment 2)

7. How did Booker T. Washington propose that African Americans respond to the conditions they faced? Why did he take this position? (text, pp. 780–781; video segment 3)

8. What actions did W.E.B. DuBois propose that African Americans take to counter discrimination? What was the essence of his message? (text, pp. 781–782; video segment 3)

9. What prompted Ida B. Wells to launch an anti-lynching campaign? What tactics did she use? What strategies did she encourage to counter discrimination and intimidation? (text, pp. 650–651; video segment 3)

10. What were the major issues facing women in the late nineteenth century? In what ways were women politically active at that time? (text, pp. 651–653; video segment 4)

11. Why was the Women's Christian Temperance Union the most important women's organization of the era? How and why did Frances Willard influence the work of the WCTU? What was the argument supporting the "home protection" ballot? (text, pp. 652, 704–706, 720–721; video segment 4)

12. What was the status of the women's suffrage movement in the late nineteenth century? (text, pp. 721–722; video segment 4)

13. What explained the emergence of the black women's club movement? What issues did these organizations address? What was the main issue dividing black and white women activists? (text, pp. 651–652; video segment 4)

14. In general, what was the legacy of the struggle for African American and women's freedom and equality in the late nineteenth century? (text, all pages; video segments 1–5)

HISTORICAL EXPERTS INTERVIEWED

Steven Hahn, Professor of History, University of Pennsylvania, Philadelphia, PA
Nancy Hewitt, Professor of History and Women's and Gender Studies, Rutgers University, New Brunswick, NJ
David Levering Lewis, Professor of History, New York University, New York, NY
Michelle Mitchell, Associate Professor, University of Michigan, Ann Arbor, MI
Jacqueline Jones Royster, Professor of English, Ohio State University, Columbus, OH

FEATURED FAMILY MEMBERS INTERVIEWED

Dianne Swann-Wright, Lake Monticello, VA
Arthur Vanderbilt, Roseland, NJ

PRACTICE TEST

The following items will help you evaluate your understanding of this lesson. Use the Answer Key at the end of the lesson to check your answers or to locate material related to each question.

Multiple Choice: Choose the letter of the best answer.

1. For African Americans, the "New South" _____.
    A. provided needed factory jobs for them
    B. appeared quite similar to the Old South
    C. enabled them to escape the hardships of sharecropping
    D. assured them of equal social opportunities

2. In the video, Professor David Levering Lewis observes that Jim Crow laws _____
    A. allowed whites to maintain power in the "New South."
    B. required equal funding for segregated schools.
    C. protected blacks from white terrorism.
    D. denied black males the right to vote.

3. In the late nineteenth century, the notion that black men were a threat to white women in the South contributed significantly to _____.
    A. the desertion of southern whites from the Democratic Party
    B. the increased participation of those women in politics
    C. the solidification of cross-racial political alliances
    D. an increase in lynchings across the South

4. One response by African Americans to the Jim Crow South was to _____.
    A. undertake mass migration back to Africa
    B. attempt to amend the Fourteenth Amendment
    C. form local associations to gain more control over their lives
    D. engage in widespread counter-terrorism activities

5. Ida B. Wells urged African Americans to take all of the following actions EXCEPT _____.
    A. publicize the horrors of lynching
    B. arm themselves
    C. migrate north
    D. accommodate oppression in the short term

6. Denied the right to vote during the late nineteenth century, American women _____.
    A. turned inward and refused to engage in the political process
    B. conceded that politics was "a man's game"
    C. affected the political process though reform movements
    D. took on a major role in presidential politics

Lesson 4—A Dream Deferred

7. By 1900, the WCTU (Women's Christian Temperance Union) could claim credit for _____.
    A. the emergence of an organized movement for woman suffrage
    B. providing a generation of women with experience in political action
    C. securing the right to vote for all women
    D. securing a constitutional amendment banning the sale and consumption of alcohol

8. In 1869, Elizabeth Cady Stanton and Susan B. Anthony formed the National Woman Suffrage Association, which _____.
    A. was the first women's group in America
    B. was the most conservative group of women in America
    C. would lobby for both voting rights and wage equalization
    D. demanded the vote for women

Short Answer: Your answers should specifically address the points indicated in one or two paragraphs.

9. What were the essential differences between approaches advocated by Booker T. Washington and W.E.B. DuBois to address issues confronting African Americans? Why did each take the position that they did?

10. Why and how did Ida B. Wells undertake an anti-lynching campaign? What did her 1892 study of lynching demonstrate about the practice?

11. What was the original purpose of the Women's Christian Temperance Union? How and why did its second president, Frances Willard, change the organization?

Essay Question: Your response should be several paragraphs long. Your answer should elaborate on the points indicated in a manner that expresses understanding of the material.

12. Why and how were African Americans and women subjected to inferior positions in American life by 1900? How did they try to change the conditions they faced? What was the legacy of their struggle for freedom and equality in the late nineteenth century?

ANSWER KEY

Answer	Learning Objectives	Focus Points	References
1. B	LO 1	FP 2	Text, pp. 649–651; video segment 2
2. A	LO 1	FP 4	Video segment 2
3. D	LO 1	FP 6	Text, pp. 650–651; video segment 2
4. C	LO 2	FP 14	Video segment 3
5. D	LO 2	FP 9	Text, pp. 650–651; video segment 3
6. C	LO 3	FP 10	Text, pp. 651–653; video segment 4
7. B	LO 3	FP 11	Text, pp. 652, 704–706, 720–721; video segment 4
8. D	LO 3	FP 12	Text, pp. 721–722; video segment 4

9. ....LO 2.................FP 7, 8 .... Text, pp. 780–782; video segment 3
   - Consider the times and issues confronting African Americans.
   - What was B.T. Washington's background? What did he say about segregation and education? What was his position on political and social equality?
   - What was W.E.B. Dubois' background? What did he say about education and obtaining equal rights?

10. ....LO 2.................FP 9 .... Text, pp. 650–651; video segment 3
    - Why was lynching occurring so often?
    - How was Ida Wells personally affected?
    - How did Wells counter popular myths about lynching?

11. ....LO 3.................FP 11 .... Text, pp. 652, 704–706, 720–721; video segment 4
    - Why was excessive drinking of alcohol an issue for women?
    - What did the WCTU propose to do about the issue?
    - What other issues did the WCTU confront under Willard's leadership?

12. ....LO 1-4...............FP 14 .... Text, all pages; video segments 1–5
    - Consider the economic, political, and social discrimination aimed at African Americans and women.
    - How was discrimination practiced?
    - Why was discrimination practiced?
    - What leaders spoke out against the discrimination? What points did they make?
    - What organizations attempted to tackle the inequities?
    - What success did the reformers have at the time? What limited their success? What were the longer-term effects of their efforts?

ENRICHMENT IDEAS

These activities are not required unless your instructor assigns them. They are offered as suggestions to help you learn more about the material presented in this lesson.

1. You are an African American living in the South in the period 1895–1905. In a well-developed 750-word essay, explain why you endorse the recommendations of Booker T. Washington, W.E.B. DuBois, or Ida B. Wells. Why do you think the approach you are following is better than the others?

2. You are a woman living in the United States in the late nineteenth century. In a well-developed 750-word essay, describe the three most important issues facing women of your era and explain how you propose to address each issue so that positive change will occur.

SUGGESTED READINGS/RESOURCES

See the "Bibliography" on pages 660–661, 700–701, 741, and 782–783 of the text if you wish to examine other books and resources related to the material discussed in this lesson.

Lesson 5

Labor's Struggle

OVERVIEW

The changes taking place in the industrializing nation in the late nineteenth century depended on the workers who built America. Those workers were plentiful, migrating from other countries and from within the United States. Like today, workers were diverse in gender, ethnicity, and the types of labor they performed. Unlike today, most workers in the late nineteenth century labored in extremely harsh conditions with little or no support systems in the workplace. Those laboring in America may have dreamed that the Horatio Alger stories would come to life for them, but those dreams disintegrated as their bodies weakened with work and age. The cold reality was that most workers had little chance to improve their plight through their individual efforts.

In response to the conditions they faced, some workers were attracted to theories promising to alter the capitalist system. Even more workers turned to national labor organizations. Because the stakes were high, unions faced strong opposition from management and their allies in government.

The gains made by workers in the late nineteenth century were few, but what they did mattered. Who were these workers? Why were their working lives so hard? What can we learn from labor's struggle?

LESSON ASSIGNMENT

Text: Roark, et.al., *The American Promise*
- Chapter 19, "The City and Its Workers," pp. 664–666, 677–688, 697, 700
- Chapter 20, "Dissent, Depression, and War," pp. 714–719

Video: "Labor's Struggle," from the series *Transforming America*

LEARNING OBJECTIVES

This lesson examines the struggle of workers to deal with harsh conditions facing labor in the late nineteenth century. Upon completion of this lesson, you should be able to:

1. Describe the composition of the work force, the nature of work, and working conditions in the late nineteenth century.

2. Analyze the formation, leadership, goals, membership, and relative success of national labor unions during this period.

3. Analyze the resistance to unions by management, governmental entities, and the general public, culminating in large-scale industrial violence.

4. Assess the status of American labor, the union movement, and the meaning of labor's struggle at the end of this era.

LESSON FOCUS POINTS

The following questions are designed to help you get the most benefit from the sources selected for this lesson. For reference purposes, the video is divided into five segments: (1) Introduction, (2) "They Dared Not Stop Working," (3) "The First Red Scare," (4) "Fight It to the Finish," and (5) Summary Analysis: "So Much Was at Stake."

1. Why did the Great Railroad Strike of 1877 take place? Why did it become violent? How did the strike end? Why was it important? (text, pp. 683–685; video segment 1)

2. Who comprised the working classes in the late nineteenth century? What types of jobs did they do? Why was child labor common? (text, pp. 677–683; video segment 2)

3. How would you describe the working conditions for most workers? Why were these conditions so harsh? How did the conditions for workers building the Brooklyn Bridge illustrate the difficulties workers faced? (text, pp. 664–666, 677–683; video segment 2)

4. Why was the business climate in the late nineteenth century so unfavorable for unions? How did socialists and anarchists propose to change this climate? Who was Oscar Neebe? Why did he become a socialist? (text, pp. 683–685; video segment 3)

5. What were the similarities and differences between the Knights of Labor and the American Federation of Labor? (text, pp. 685–686; video segment 3)

6. Why was the eight-hour day such a rallying cry for labor in the 1880s? How was the eight-hour day movement connected to events in Chicago in May, 1886? (text, pp. 686–687; video segment 3)

7. How and why did violence erupt at Haymarket Square in Chicago on May 4, 1886? What were the consequences of the "Haymarket riot" (Haymarket Affair)? (text, pp. 687–688; video segments 3, 5)

8. What prompted the Homestead Lockout in 1892? Why did violence break out? What issues were at stake? How was this dispute resolved? What were the consequences? (text, pp. 714–716; video segment 4)

9. Why did miners go on strike in Cripple Creek, Colorado, in 1894? What was unusual about this strike? How was it resolved? Why is it significant? (text, pp. 716–717)

10. Why was Pullman, Illinois, a "company town?" Why did workers strike against the Pullman Palace Car Company in 1894? (text, pp. 717–719; video segment 4)

11. Why did the Pullman strike become national? What issues were at stake? What role did Eugene Debs play? (text, 718–719; video segment 4)

12. How was the Pullman Strike broken? What were the consequences? Why did Eugene Debs turn to socialism? (text, pp. 718–719; video segment 4)

13. In summary, how and why did workers engage in collective action against their employers in the late nineteenth century? What limited their success? What issues were at stake? What is the legacy of labor's struggle during that era? (text, all pages; video segments 1–5)

HISTORICAL EXPERTS INTERVIEWED

Eric Arneson, Professor of History and African American Studies, University of Illinois, Chicago, IL
Sarah Stage, Professor, Arizona State University, West Campus, Phoenix, AZ
Howard Zinn, Professor Emeritus, Boston University, Boston, MA

FEATURED FAMILY MEMBER INTERVIEWED

Bill Neebe, Wilmette, IL

PRACTICE TEST

The following items will help you evaluate your understanding of this lesson. Use the Answer Key at the end of the lesson to check your answers or to locate material related to each question.

Multiple Choice: Choose the letter of the best answer.

1. Workers in industrial America in the 1880s and 1890s _____.
    A. tended to be wage earners rather than independent artisans
    B. had to be skilled in order to get a job
    C. faced a declining need for their labor
    D. were similar to pre-Civil War laborers in number and types

2. In the working-class family of nineteenth-century America, economic survival _____.
    A. depended on everyone working
    B. was assured if the head of household was able to find a job
    C. was assured if both parents worked outside the home
    D. required the assistance of social service agencies

3. In the late nineteenth century, most business managers viewed their workers as _____.
   A. worthy of safe and healthy work environments
   B. expendable commodities who could easily be replaced
   C. radical anarchists threatening their property
   D. equal partners in the decision-making process

4. The main lesson workers learned from the Great Railroad Strike of 1877 was that _____.
   A. concerted action was effective
   B. they could not fight corporations
   C. strikes received little attention from authorities
   D. higher wages could easily be obtained

5. In its approach to union organization, the Knights of Labor officially _____.
   A. encouraged use of the violence
   B. stressed organization of workers by craft
   C. discriminated against blacks and women
   D. welcomed both skilled and unskilled workers

6. The Haymarket Affair of 1886 _____.
   A. began as a rally of laborers organized by radicals
   B. took place in Boston
   C. involved railroad workers who were dissatisfied with their wages
   D. made the Knights of Labor more powerful than ever

7. The workers' strike at the Homestead plant in 1892 was fundamentally _____.
   A. a contest between workers' rights and property rights
   B. an attempt by workers to take over the management of the plant
   C. a personal attack on Andrew Carnegie
   D. an attack on Henry Clay Frick's management policies

8. The primary issue that triggered the Cripple Creek miners' strike of 1894 was the _____.
   A. miners' demand that workers should own the gold mines
   B. owners' efforts to lengthen the workday from eight to ten hours
   C. outcome of Colorado's gubernatorial election in 1892
   D. miners' demand for higher wages

9. All of the following are associated with the Pullman Strike EXCEPT _____.
   A. wages were cut, but rents for housing were not reduced
   B. an injunction was used against the workers
   C. federal troops moved the mail and broke the strike
   D. the American Railway Union emerged stronger

10. The video "Labor's Struggle" points out that in addition to wages and conditions, the strikes and labor disputes of the late nineteenth century were about _____.
    A. government ownership of factories
    B. freedom of the press
    C. inheritance taxes on the wealthy
    D. dignity for workers

Short Answer: Your answer should specifically address the points indicated in one or two paragraphs.

11. Why did the Great Railroad Strike of 1877 take place? Why was it a tuning point in labor history?

12. What were the major differences between the Knights of Labor and the American Federation of Labor? Why were the differences important?

13. Why did the Haymarket Affair happen? What were the consequences of this event?

14. Why did Eugene V. Debs become a socialist after the Pullman Strike? Why was his rejection of capitalism a moral issue?

Essay Question: Your response should be several paragraphs long. Your answer should elaborate on the points indicated in a manner that expresses understanding of the material.

15. How and why did workers engage in collective action against their employers in the last quarter of the nineteenth century? What limited their success? What issues were at stake? What is the legacy of labor's struggle during that era?

ANSWER KEY

	Answer	Learning Objectives	Focus Points	References
1.	A	LO 1	FP 2	Text, pp. 677–683; video segment 2
2.	A	LO 1	FP 2	Text, pp. 677–683; video segment 2
3.	B	LO 1	FP 3	Text, pp. 664–666, 677–683; video segment 2
4.	A	LO 3	FP 1	Text, pp. 683–685; video segment 1
5.	D	LO 2	FP 5	Text, pp. 685–686; video segment 3
6.	A	LO 3	FP 6, 7	Text, pp. 686–688; video segment 3
7.	A	LO 3	FP 8	Text, pp. 714–716; video segment 4
8.	B	LO 3	FP 9	Text, pp. 716–717
9.	D	LO 3	FP 10, 11	Text, pp. 717–719; video segment 4
10.	D	LO 4	FP 13	Video segment 5

11. ....LO 3.....................FP 1 .... Text, pp. 683–685; video segment 1
    - Consider the wages, hours, and working conditions.
    - How did management and upper classes respond?
    - What did workers learn from the experience?

12. ....LO 2.....................FP 5 .... Text, pp. 685–686; video segment 3
    - Who was eligible to join the Knights? What were its goals?
    - How was the AFL organized? What issues did it consider most important?
    - Which organization emerged stronger? Why?

13. ....LO 3.....................FP 6, 7 .... Text, pp. 686–687; video segments 3, 5
    - Consider the events of the previous three days.
    - What role did the police play? Why did they act as they did?
    - Why were anarchists held responsible? How did it affect the labor movement?

14. ....LO 4.....................FP 12 .... Text, pp. 718–719; video segment 4
    - How and why did the government help break the strike?
    - Why did he reject capitalism on moral grounds?
    - Why did he think socialism was a better alternative?

15. ....LO 1–4..................FP 13 .... Text, all pages; all video segments
    - Consider the wages, hours, and working conditions for most factory workers.
    - Why did individual workers have little or no power at this time?
    - What major strikes took place? What were the results?
    - Consider how the availability of strikebreakers, the power of corporate managers, the agencies of government, and the culture limited the success of unions.
    - To what extent were workers standing up for their dignity?
    - What lessons were learned from labor's struggle in that era?

ENRICHMENT IDEAS

These activities are not required unless your instructor assigns them. They are offered as suggestions to help you learn more about the material presented in this lesson.

1. You are a union organizer in the late nineteenth century trying to persuade workers to join the union. In a well-developed position paper, present your best case for membership.

2. If you are not a union member, interview someone who is, asking him or her to cite his or her reasons for belonging to the union. Then write a report summarizing your findings and stating your own conclusions about union workers.

3. If you are a union member, interview someone who is not, asking him or her to cite his or her reasons for not belonging to a union. Then write a report summarizing your findings and stating your conclusions about nonunion workers.

SUGGESTED READINGS/RESOURCES

See the "Bibliography "on pages 700–701 and 741 of the text if you wish to examine other books and resources related to the material discussed in this lesson.

Lesson 6

The Populist Challenge

OVERVIEW

The industrializing process that took place in the United States in the late nineteenth century brought together concentrations of people, resources, wealth, and power. In a country with a political system that is supposed to represent the majority, the exercise of extraordinary political power by the few raised some fundamental and timeless questions. Who were the politicians and the major political parties really representing? Why and how had political power gravitated toward the rich business class? What could be done about it?

For most of the late nineteenth century, national politicians enacted and implemented government policies and practices highly favorable to big business. Meanwhile, worker dissatisfaction had prompted the emergence of unions, which were most often busted by a combination of management and government power. At the same time, farmers became increasingly aware that they could not control their own destiny. Ironically, perhaps, the "independent" yeomen turned to collective action to demand change.

Since neither the Republican nor Democratic Party responded adequately to their needs, the disgruntled farmers led the formation of a third party. By 1892, the Populist (or People's) Party was challenging the prevailing theories of Social Darwinism and laissez-faire government. As one historian has observed, "it was the corporate state that the People's Party attempted to bring under democratic control."

The Populist challenge reached a climax in the 1896 presidential election. When the Democrats absorbed most of their proposals and nominated William Jennings Bryan to take on the Republican William McKinley, the Populists fused with the Democrats. When McKinley and corporate America won, the Populists were dead as a political party. But their legacy remained. They had identified fundamental issues and proposed political intervention to deal with them. The issues would not die, and many of their proposed solutions would be implemented in the twentieth century.

LESSON ASSIGNMENT

Text: Roark, et.al., *The American Promise*
- Chapter 18, "Business and Politics in the Gilded Age," pp. 626–628, 645–660
- Chapter 20, "Dissent, Depression, and War," pp. 704–713, 722–727, 740

Video: "The Populist Challenge" from the series *Transforming America*

LEARNING OBJECTIVES

This lesson examines the development, meaning, and legacy of the Populist challenge to the established political powers of the era. Upon completion of this lesson, you should be able to:

1. Explain the characteristics of national politics during the late nineteenth century.

2. Analyze the economic and political issues troubling rural Americans during this era.

3. Explain how agrarian reformers addressed the major issues through the Farmers' Alliance movement.

4. Analyze the rise and fall of the Populist Party.

5. Assess the legacy of the Populists.

LESSON FOCUS POINTS

The following questions are designed to help you get the most benefit from the sources selected for this lesson. For reference purposes, the video is divided into five segments: (1) Introduction, (2) "A Bare Hard Living," (3) "The Farmers' Alliance," (4) "The People's Party," and (5) Summary Analysis: "The Populist Legacy."

1. How would you characterize the political culture in the Gilded Age? Why was voter turnout high? How and why was party affiliation and loyalty important? What roles did religion and ethnicity play? (text, pp. 626–628, 647–649)

2. Why was political corruption and party factionalism common during this era? How was this illustrated? (text, pp. 653–654)

3. Why was the Pendleton Civil Service Act passed in 1883? Why was it important? (text, pp. 654–655)

4. How did the presidential election of 1884 illustrate the politics of the era? (text, pp. 626, 655–656)

5. How were issues surrounding the tariff, business regulation, and national currency being addressed? What were the political ramifications of these economic issues? (text, pp. 656–659)

6. How and why could *The Wizard of Oz* be interpreted as a political parable or allegory? (video segment 1)

7. What were the major economic and political problems facing farmers in the late nineteenth century? Whom did they blame for their troubles? (text, pp. 704–707; video segment 2)

8. Why did the Farmers' Alliance movement grow in the 1880s? How did the alliances initially

address the issues confronting farmers, including black farmers? Who opposed their efforts? (pp. 707–710; video segment 3)

9. Why did the Farmers' Alliance become political? What happened at the St. Louis convention in February 1892? (text, pp. 705–706, 710–711; video segment 3)

10. What were the main planks in the Populist Party (Omaha) Platform of 1892? How did these proposals challenge the political and economic establishment? (text, pp. 710–713; video segment 4)

11. How and why did the Populists reach out to the working classes of the city and across racial lines? What political success did they have in 1892? (text, pp. 724–725; video segment 4)

12. Why was the Populist coalition with African Americans a threat to the southern political order? How did the populists' opponents in the South react? (text, pp. 724–725; video segment 4)

13. How did the economic depression of 1893-1894 affect national politics? What was important about Coxey's "army?" (text, pp. 659–660, 722–725; video segment 4)

14. How and why did the Democrats create a dilemma for the Populists in 1896? Why was fusion a difficult decision for the Populists? What does this illustrate about third parties in American politics? (text, pp. 725–727; video segment 4)

15. Explain the presidential election of 1896 in terms of candidates, issues, campaign, and results. Why did "free silver" take on such importance? What was at stake in this election? Why did McKinley win? What did his victory mean? (text, pp. 724–727; video segment 4)

16. In summary, what factors explain the emergence of the Populist movement? Why and how did the Populists challenge the political establishment of the late nineteenth century? What is the legacy of the Populists and of populism? (text, all pages; video segments 2–5)

HISTORICAL EXPERTS INTERVIEWED

Omar Ali, Assistant Professor of History, Towson University, Towson, MD
H.W. Brands, Professor of History, University of Texas, Austin, TX
Steven Hahn, Professor of History, University of Pennsylvania, Philadelphia, PA
Michael Kazin, Professor of History, Georgetown University, Washington, DC
Sarah Stage, Professor, Arizona State University, West Campus, Phoenix, AZ

FEATURED FAMILY MEMBERS INTERVIEWED

Charlene McAden, Blooming Grove, TX
Irene Lafferty Logan, Garber, OK
Dianne Swann-Wright, Lake Monticello, VA

PRACTICE TEST

The following items will help you evaluate your understanding of this lesson. Use the Answer Key at the end of the lesson to check your answers or to locate material related to each question.

Multiple Choice: Choose the letter of the best answer.

1. Voter turnout in national elections during the last three decades of the nineteenth century averaged 80 percent, a phenomenon that can be attributed in part to the _____.
   A. incredible popularity of the candidates who ran for president
   B. fact that most Americans were very knowledgeable about the issues of the day
   C. fact that voting was an important way to get a government job
   D. belief that participating in politics was a moral obligation

2. In the last decades of the nineteenth century, national politics in the United States was dominated by _____.
   A. civil service reformers
   B. a series of strong chief executives
   C. the Democrats
   D. dynamic party bosses

3. President James A. Garfield unwittingly helped the cause of civil service reform when he _____.
   A. mistakenly signed a legislative act enabling that reform
   B. was shot by Charles Guiteau, a disappointed office seeker
   C. made a series of speeches that appeared to endorse government reforms
   D. refused to speak out on standardizing the requirements for federal jobs.

4. The Interstate Commerce Commission, the nation's first federal regulatory agency, was _____.
   A. so weak in its early years that it served as little more than an historical precedent
   B. had unprecedented power to clean up and regulate the railroads
   C. authorized to set interest rates for small-business loans
   D. so powerful initially that the Supreme Court declared it unconstitutional

5. For farmers, the crop lien system _____.
   A. provided a way to borrow feed for livestock
   B. resulted in an inflated currency
   C. lowered prices for farm machinery
   D. left them in perpetual debt

6. The Southern Farmers' Alliance and the Colored Farmers' Alliance _____.
   A. had total disregard for each other's interests
   B. disagreed on some issues but attempted to make common cause on others
   C. were in total agreement and worked together harmoniously
   D. found common cause in the struggle to end racism

7. A gathering in St. Louis in February 1892, which evolved into the People's Party, was attended by _____.
   A. loyal Republicans and Democrats
   B. Democrats who wanted to regain power in the South
   C. farmers, labor leaders, women's leaders, and others who wanted change
   D. third-party dissidents with ties to Russian revolutionaries

8. The Populist Party platform (1892) advocated all of the following EXCEPT _____.
   A. more direct democracy
   B. minimum wages for farm workers
   C. a graduated income tax
   D. government ownership of railroads

9. As the election of 1896 approached, the depression worsened, and rebellion was brewing in the ranks of both Democrats and Republicans over the issue of _____.
   A. crop prices
   B. free silver
   C. labor reforms
   D. controlling trusts

10. One of the legacies of populism is the recognition that democracy _____.
    A. gives everyone real political power
    B. assures all classes are represented
    C. faces a problem with inequalities in society
    D. protects the rights of minorities

Short Answer: Your answer should specifically address the points indicated in one or two paragraphs.

11. Why and how did the Farmers' Alliance become more political in the 1880s and early 1890s?

12. Why did the Populist Party reach out to black voters in the 1890s? What were the results of their efforts?

13. Why is the presidential election of 1896 important in American political history?

Essay Question: Your response should be several paragraphs long and elaborate on the points indicated in a manner that expresses understanding of the material.

14. Explain the emergence of the Populist movement in the late nineteenth century. Why and how did the Populist Party challenge the political establishment? What is the legacy of the Populists and of populism?

ANSWER KEY

	Answer	Learning Objectives	Focus Points	References
1.	C	LO 1	FP 1	Text, pp. 647–649
2.	D	LO 1	FP 2	Text, pp. 653–654
3.	B	LO 1	FP 3	Text, pp. 654–655
4.	A	LO 1	FP 5	Text, pp. 656–659
5.	D	LO 2	FP 7	Text, pp. 704–707; video segment 2
6.	B	LO 3	FP 8	Text, pp. 707–710
7.	C	LO 4	FP 9	Text, pp. 705–706, 710–711; video segment 3
8.	B	LO 4	FP 10	Text, pp. 710–713; video segment 4
9.	B	LO 4	FP 15	Text, pp. 724–727; video segment 4
10.	C	LO 5	FP 16	Video segment 5

11. .... LO 3, 4 .... FP 9 .... Text, pp. 705–706, 710–711; video segment 3
   - What had happened to their economic initiatives?
   - How did the major parties respond to their issues?
   - What steps were taken to form a third party? What did it stand for?

12. .... LO 4 .... FP 11, 12 .... Text, pp. 724–725; video segment 4
   - Consider the common interests of white and black farmers.
   - Why would black politicians and voters be attracted to a third party?
   - What success did they have? How did their opponents react?

13. .... LO 4 .... FP 15 .... Text, pp. 724–727; video segment 4
   - What was at stake in this election?
   - How did the election affect politics and parties?
   - What did the results indicate?

14. .... LO 1–5 .... FP 16 .... Text, all pages; video segment 2–5
   - Consider the economic problems faced by farmers.
   - How did the Farmers' Alliance address issues? What success did it have?
   - Why was the Populist Party formed? What reforms did it advocate?
   - Why was the political and economic establishment threatened by the Populists?
   - How did the Populists influence later reforms and reformers?
   - Why does "populism" take on a meaning of its own? What does it mean?

ENRICHMENT IDEAS

These activities are not required unless your instructor assigns them. They are offered as suggestions to help you learn more about the material presented in this lesson.

1. Read the "Documenting the American Promise" feature on "Populist Voices of Protest" on pages 712–713 of the text. In a well-developed essay, answer the questions posed in the text, comment on the effectiveness of these "voices," and reflect on how protest is voiced in our times.

2. Research the history of third parties in the United States since 1877. Using three third parties as examples, submit a report in which you evaluate their importance in American political history.

3. Whom would you have voted for in the 1896 presidential election? Submit a thoughtful essay in which you explain your position.

SUGGESTED READINGS/RESOURCES

See the "Bibliography" on pages 660–661 and 741 of the text if you wish to examine other books and resources related to the material discussed in this lesson.

Lesson 7

The Question of Empire

OVERVIEW

Prior to the 1890s, the American people and their leaders had been primarily concerned with the dynamic internal affairs that were transforming the nation. However, by the end of that decade, the United States had fought its first overseas war and decided to engage in imperialism well beyond its national boundaries. Why had this happened? What did it mean to America and to the world?

The Spanish-American War of 1898 provides an excellent opportunity to examine the question of why nations go to war, especially when no vital interest is at stake. Some of the same forces that began drawing Americans to the outside world came to a head in Cuba. Events there provided the immediate causes for a declared war against Spain. Was this a necessary war? Was it justified? What were its consequences?

When the U.S. Senate considered the ratification of the treaty ending the war, senators debated some fundamental questions about the role of the United States in the world. Essentially the same questions, many of which involve a tense mixture of self-interest and idealism, are still being discussed in our times.

Once the decision had been made to broaden the boundaries of an American empire, the United States faced the challenges inherent in being an imperialist nation and a world power. Suppression of an indigenous rebellion against American control of the Philippines led to an undeclared war more costly than the previous conflict with Spain. Application of the "big stick" in Latin America led to political, economic, and military intervention by the United States.

Indeed, the active participation of the United States in world affairs at the turn of the twentieth century forever transformed America and much of the world. What were the costs and benefits of America's emergence as a major player on the world stage?

LESSON ASSIGNMENT

Text: Roark, et. al., *The American Promise*
- Chapter 20, "Dissent, Depression, and War," pp. 727–743
- Chapter 21, "Progressivism from the Grass Roots to the White House," pp. 765, 768–771

Video: "The Question of Empire," from the series *Transforming America*

LEARNING OBJECTIVES

This lesson examines the causes and consequences of American involvement in world affairs at the turn of the twentieth century. Upon completion of this lesson, you should be able to:

1. Explain the factors that contributed to a shift in American foreign policy in the late nineteenth century.

2. Analyze the causes and consequences of the Spanish-American War.

3. Analyze the reasons for and against American imperialism.

4. Assess the costs and benefits of American involvement in Asia and Latin America during the late nineteenth and early twentieth centuries.

5. Assess how the developments of this era transformed America and its place in the world.

LESSON FOCUS POINTS

The following questions are designed to help you get the most benefit from the sources selected for this lesson. For reference purposes, the video is divided into five segments: (1) Introduction, (2) "A Splendid Little War," (3) "Heel of Achilles," (4) "The Big Stick," and (5) Summary Analysis: "Beyond American Boundaries."

1. How did American involvement in Hawaii in the 1890s illustrate U.S. interests in the Pacific region and the emerging struggle in American foreign policy? (text, pp. 728, 730–731; video segment 1)

2. Why did Americans begin to take more interest in foreign affairs in the late nineteenth century? How important were markets and missionaries in this development? How were these two factors connected? What did the Boxer Rebellion indicate about the connection? (text, pp. 727–731; video segment 2)

3. How and why were the Monroe Doctrine and the Open Door policy the "twin pillars" of American expansionist foreign policy in the late nineteenth and early twentieth centuries? (text, pp. 729, 732–733)

4. What were the underlying causes of the Spanish-American War? What national interests were at stake in Cuba? How important were economic, strategic, and humanitarian interests? What role did the press play? (text, pp. 733–734; video segment 2)

5. How critical was President William McKinley in this process of going to war? Why was he initially cautious in approaching the Cuban situation? Why is he referred to as "the first modern American president?" (video segment 2)

6. Why was the American battleship *Maine* sent to Cuba? Why did it explode and sink in the Havana harbor? What were the consequences? Why does McKinley finally decide to go to war? (text, 734–737; video segment 2)

7. Why did the American people respond to the Spanish-American War? Why was it referred to as "a splendid little war?" Was it a necessary war? Why was it important? (text, pp. 734–735; video segment 2)

8. What were the terms of the Treaty of Paris (1898)? Why was the Senate debate on its ratification so important? (text, 735, 738–741; video segment 3)

9. What were the main arguments of those favoring (pro) and those opposing (anti) imperialism? Why did the Senate ratify the Treaty of Paris? Why did that decision transform the United States? (text, pp. 738–741; video segment 3)

10. How was the relationship of Cuba and Hawaii with the United States altered by the events surrounding the Spanish-American War? (text, pp. 738–741)

11. Why did a Filipino-American war break out in 1899? What were the consequences of this conflict? Why did the Philippines become America's "heel of Achilles?" (text, pp. 738–741; video segment 3)

12. How did President Theodore Roosevelt perceive the role of the United States in the world? What did his fondness for the proverb, "speak softly and carry a big stick," indicate about his approach to foreign affairs? (text 765, 768–769; video segment 4)

13. What actions did Theodore Roosevelt take in reference to Asia and Europe? How did his actions in these regions reflect his sense of the balance and limits of power? (text, pp. 765, 768–769; video segment 4)

14. How and why did President Theodore Roosevelt intervene in Panama to secure the rights to build a canal? Why did the Panama Canal open a whole new chapter in American foreign policy? (text, pp. 768–769; video segment 4)

15. What is the Roosevelt Corollary to the Monroe Doctrine? Why is it important? (text, p. 769; video segment 4)

16. Why and how did President William Howard Taft pursue "dollar diplomacy?" What were the results of this policy? (text, p. 771)

17. In summary, why and how were the relations of the United States with the rest of the world transformed during this era? What were the consequences of that transformation? How is what happened then connected to the world of today? (text, all pages; video segments 1–5)

HISTORICAL EXPERTS INTERVIEWED

H.W. Brands, Professor of History, University of Texas, Austin, TX
Walter LaFeber, Professor of History, Cornell University, Ithaca, NY
Sarah Stage, Professor, Arizona State University, West Campus, Phoenix, AZ
John Stoessinger, Distinguished Professor of International Affairs, University of San Diego, San Diego, CA

FEATURED FAMILY MEMBER INTERVIEWED

Edward Archuleta, Santa Fe, NM

PRACTICE TEST

The following items will help you evaluate your understanding of this lesson. Use the Answer Key at the end of the lesson to check your answers or to locate material related to each question.

Multiple Choice: Choose the letter of the best answer.

1. Some Americans became enthused about annexing Hawaii in the 1890s because of interest in _____.
    A. commerce and naval bases
    B. democracy and rule of law
    C. equality and freedom
    D. all of the above

2. In addition to economic motivations, a factor that contributed significantly to U.S. expansion overseas in the 1890s was _____.
    A. Christian missionaries' eagerness to spread the gospel
    B. Americans' interest in new religions and cultures
    C. the federal government's commitment to promote cultural understanding
    D. the federal government's plan to provoke religious conflict in Asia

3. Secretary of State John Hay initiated the Open Door policy in 1900 to ensure _____.
    A. trade between the United States and Africa
    B. trade between the United States and Latin America
    C. that immigrants from Asia could enter the United States
    D. access to trade in China for all

4. When Theodore Roosevelt said the United States "needs" a war, he expressed a view held by those people who _____.
   A. fought in the Civil War
   B. lost loved ones in the Filipino Insurrection
   C. came to maturity in the 1880s and 1890s
   D. supported intervention in the Russian revolution

5. America's entrance into the Spanish–American War was a direct result of _____.
   A. Spain's attack on Florida
   B. the sinking of the *Maine*
   C. Spain's border dispute with Venezuela
   D. the nation's wanting to colonize Cuba

6. William McKinley is considered by some historians to be the first "modern" president because of the way he controlled _____.
   A. the press
   B. his cabinet
   C. Congress
   D. the Supreme Court

7. The U.S. Senate's debate on the ratification of the Treaty of Paris, which officially ended the Spanish-American war, was important because it _____.
   A. concerned Democratic efforts to use a filibuster to block the vote
   B. indicated an improper use of checks and balances
   C. exposed the duplicity of the McKinley administration
   D. involved the decision to establish an American empire

8. U.S. control of the Philippines did not come easy because _____.
   A. U.S. business interests saw no reason to develop markets in that part of the world
   B. Congress did not want any part of it
   C. revolutionaries fought against the United States for seven years
   D. a majority of people in the United States at the time were against imperialism

9. The Roosevelt Corollary to the Monroe Doctrine _____.
   A. set up the United States as the police power in the Western Hemisphere
   B. relaxed the doctrine's restrictions on European nations
   C. worked so well that the United States has never found it necessary to send troops to any nation in Latin America
   D. was inconsistent with the president's overall foreign policy

10. As a result of the emergence of the United States as a major power in world affairs in the late nineteenth and early twentieth centuries, _____.
    A. European nations became more willing to settle disputes peacefully
    B. Japan accepted a secondary role in Asian affairs
    C. Latin American countries gained more freedom
    D. America often ignored the "inalienable rights" of other peoples

Short Answer: Your answer should specifically address the points indicated in one or two paragraphs.

11. Do you think the Spanish-American War was necessary? Why or why not? Why was it important?

12. What was important about the Filipino-American war? Why was it referred to as America's "heel of Achilles?"

13. How did the United States use a "big stick" policy in Latin America in the early twentieth century? What were the results?

Essay Question: Your response should be several paragraphs long and elaborate on the points indicated in a manner that expresses understanding of the material.

14. How and why were the relations of the United States with the rest of the world transformed in the late nineteenth and early twentieth centuries? What were the consequences of that transformation? How is what happened then connected to the world of today?

ANSWER KEY

Answer	Learning Objectives	Focus Points	References
1. A	LO 1	FP 1	Text, pp. 728, 730–731; video segment 1
2. A	LO 1	FP 2	Text, pp. 727–731; video segment 2
3. D	LO 1	FP 3	Text, pp. 729, 732–733
4. C	LO 2	FP 4	Video segment 2
5. B	LO 2	FP 4, 6	Text, pp. 733–737; video segment 2
6. C	LO 2	FP 5	Video segment 2
7. D	LO 3	FP 8	Text, pp. 735, 738–741; video segment 3
8. C	LO 4	FP 11	Text, pp. 738–741; video segment 3
9. A	LO 4	FP 15	Text, p. 769; video segment 4
10. D	LO 5	FP 17	Video segment 5

11. LO 2 ... FP 4-6 ... Text, pp. 733–737; video segment 2
    - Take one side of the issue and defend it.
    - Consider the reasons the United States went to war. Was a vital interest at stake?
    - What were the consequences of the war?

12. LO 4 ... FP 11 ... Text, pp. 738–741; video segment 3
    - Consider the cost of the war in lives and treasure.
    - How did it preview similar situations?
    - Why did the United States lose its innocence regarding imperialism?
    - What does the "heel of Achilles" reference mean?

13. .... LO 4......................FP 14-16................................. Text, pp. 768–771; video segment 4
    - What did the "big stick" mean in that era?
    - How did American actions in Cuba and Panama reflect U.S. power?
    - What was the Roosevelt Corollary? What did "dollar diplomacy" entail?

14. .... LO 5......................FP 17...................................... Text, all pages; video segments 1–5
    - Consider the factors that explain why the United States was looking outward.
    - How did the situation with Hawaii illustrate the issues at stake?
    - How and why did the Spanish-American War affect American diplomacy?
    - What were the consequences of the decision to engage in imperialism?
    - How did the "big stick" policy affect relations with Latin America?
    - What was the place of the United States in the world? How did Americans view the world?
    - Consider the on-going issues of spreading democracy and capitalism and the uses of force.

ENRICHMENT IDEAS

These activities are not required unless your instructor assigns them. They are offered as suggestions to help you learn more about the material presented in this lesson.

1. Read the "Historical Question" feature entitled "Did Terrorists Sink the *Maine*?" on pages 736–737 of the textbook. Then submit a well-developed essay in which you (a) summarize its main points, and (b) compare and contrast the *Maine* incident and its consequences with the terrorist attacks on America on September 11, 2001.

2. You are a member of the Senate of the United States Congress in the spring of 1898. You have just voted on the declaration of war against Spain. Write a thoughtful essay in which you explain to your constituents the reasons you voted as you did.

3. You are a Filipino nationalist in 1899. Write a well-developed essay, directed at an American audience, in which you express your views on the actions of the United States in the Philippines and your recommendations to U.S. policymakers.

SUGGESTED READINGS/RESOURCES

See the "Bibliography" on pages 741 and 782–783 of the text if you wish to examine other books and resources related to the material discussed in this lesson.

 # Unit I: Fiction and Film

For further enrichment, try reading a novel or watching a film about this period of American history. Although movies and books do not always stick to historical fact, they can give a wonderful flavor of what it might have been like to live, love, work and struggle in times gone by.

Recommended novels and films set in the late nineteenth and early twentieth centuries:

Gardens in the Dunes, by Leslie Marmon Silko. A novel that moves with extraordinary fluidity and grace between the timeless, "traditional" world of American Indian peoples and the elaborate, stylized world of American upper-class culture, at the height of the Gilded Age.

Sister Carrie, by Theodore Dreiser. Dreiser's revolutionary first novel, about an eighteen-year-old country girl who moves to Chicago and becomes a kept woman. An astute, non-moralizing account of a woman and her limited options in late-nineteenth-century America.

The Age of Innocence, by Edith Wharton. Wharton's story of the upper classes of Old New York, and Newland Archer's impossible love for the disgraced Countess Olenska, is a perfectly wrought book about an era when upper-class society had rules as rigid as any in history.

The House Behind the Cedars, by Charles W. Chestnutt. First published in 1900, *The House Behind the Cedars* explores the lives and fates of two young African Americans who "pass" for white in the post-Civil War South. This book reveals how the legacy of slavery endures in racism, segregation and cultural division.

Little Big Man, d. Arthur Penn. A centenarian, the only white survivor of the Battle of Little Big Horn, shares his story in this tall tale of the Old West. Moving back and forth between the white and Indian worlds, Jack Crabb is a gunslinger, a snake-oil salesman, and an Army scout, befriending everyone from Wild Bill Hickock to General Custer. A solid blend of comedy and tragedy, with a lot to say about America's treatment of American Indians.

The Ballad of Gregorio Cortez, d. Robert M. Young. This gripping adventure film recounts the true story of the largest manhunt in Texas history. In June 1901, six hundred Texas Rangers chased Gregorio Cortez, a Mexican American ranch hand, for eleven days across 450 miles of terrain. Was Cortez a cold-blooded killer or an innocent man fleeing injustice? You decide.

Days of Heaven, d. Terence Malick. This lyrical story chronicles a trio of working-class protagonists from the steel mills of Chicago to the pastoral wheat fields of the Texas Panhandle, during a time of growing industrialization. A classic love triangle plays out to its inevitably bitter end, in this exquisite film of exceptional visual beauty.

Matewan, d. John Sayles. A little-known chapter of American labor history is brought vividly to life in this period drama. It is a fictional story about a West Virginia coal miners' strike, but every detail is so right that the film has the unmistakable ring of truth. The miners are joined by black and Italian workers who initially resist the strike, and a fateful battle ensues when detectives hired by the coal company attempt to evict miners from company housing.

Unit II

Modernizing America
1900–1945
"Freedom from Fear?"

8. The Progressive Paradox
9. A War to End All Wars
10. Modern Times
11. The Great Depression
12. A New Deal
13. Road to War
14. World at War

THEME

Americans living during the first forty-five years of the twentieth century experienced an era of triumph and tragedy. Both at home and abroad, they were helping transform a nation and a world that appear quite familiar to contemporary Americans.

    Domestically, the efforts of the progressives to smooth some of the sharper edges of industrial capitalism highlighted the early part of the century. As an emerging world power, the United States became deeply embroiled in world affairs, including the "Great" War which ended in 1918. The modern times of the 1920s brought new freedoms and heightened some old fears. Soon the Great Depression raised some fundamental questions about the American economic system. Out of the depths of that economic and social despair came one of the most sweeping political reform movements in American history. President Franklin D. Roosevelt and the New Dealers sought to alleviate fears with a support system largely still in place today. Meanwhile, the horrors of another war were brought to the United States at Pearl Harbor. Winning World War II was costly, but it ended the economic depression and thrust the nation into a world leadership role it could not reject. Freedoms were maintained, but fears persisted.

Lesson 8

The Progressive Paradox

OVERVIEW

In the opening segment of the video for this lesson, we have the opportunity to join our recurring experts as they reflect upon how American identity, freedom, and equality changed in the last quarter of the nineteenth century. While America may have been better positioned to spread its influence abroad, American identity at home was "up for grabs." Recent experience also had led many reformers to question whether an unregulated economy would really bring about greater freedom and equality in America.

At the dawn of the twentieth century, the American people lived in a nation wrought by division. Industrialization, immigration, and urbanization had sharpened the edges of capitalist society. The patriotic fervor of the Spanish-American War had diverted attention from the splits between farm and city, old and new immigrants, whites and blacks, rich and poor. But these social divisions were still present, and interclass strife was a real possibility.

Enter the progressives. During the first two decades of the twentieth century, these largely middle-class reformers attempted to confront the issues of industrial capitalism. Their proposals to alter the course of America were multi-dimensional, complex, and often paradoxical. Who were the progressives? Why and how did they transform America?

LESSON ASSIGNMENT

Text: Roark, et. al., *The American Promise*
- Chapter 21, "Progressivism from the Grass Roots to the White House," pp. 744–785

Video: "The Progressive Paradox," from the series *Transforming America*

LEARNING OBJECTIVES

This lesson examines how and why American identity, freedom, and equality had changed since 1876 and how the progressives transformed America during the early part of the twentieth century. Upon completion of this lesson, you should be able to:

1. Assess the status of American identity, freedom, and equality in 1900.

2. Describe who the progressives were and why they approached issues as they did.

3. Analyze the actions taken by progressives at the local and state levels.

4. Analyze the success of the progressives in addressing the major national issues of the era.

5. Evaluate the legacy of the progressives.

LESSON FOCUS POINTS

The following questions are designed to help you get the most benefit from the sources selected for this lesson. For reference purposes, the video is divided into five segments: (1) Introduction/Unit II Open, (2) "The Radical Center," (3) "Laboratories for Change," (4) "The Square Deal," and (5) Summary Analysis: "A Society Built on Capitalism."

1. How and why had American identity as a nation changed by 1900? Why was American identity at home "up for grabs"? (video segment 1)

2. What were the key questions revolving around American freedom and equality at the beginning of the twentieth century? (video segment 1)

3. What is the profile of the progressives? Why were women so active in the progressive movement? What motivated the progressives? What were their goals and objectives? (text, pp. 745–747; video segment 2)

4. Why did Jane Addams become involved in progressive reform? How did the work at Hull House and other settlement houses illustrate the work of progressives at the local level? Why did Addams turn to politics? What is her legacy? (text, pp. 745–749; video segment 2)

5. What was the social gospel? How did the social purity movement attack vice? Who was Margaret Sanger? What did she attempt to do? How did Sanger and her work illustrate one of the paradoxes of progressivism? (text, pp., 747–749, 777–778; video segment 2)

6. How did W.E.B. DuBois personify the progressive profile? How did DuBois, the Niagra Movement, and the NAACP try to secure rights for African Americans? Why did so many other progressives favor segregation? (text, pp. 777–782; video segment 2)

7. How and why could progressives be radical and centrist at the same time? (video segment 2)

8. How would you describe the relationship between the progressives and the working class? Why and how did the Women's Trade Union League and the National Consumers League support workers? (text, pp. 749–754)

9. What was "protective legislation?" Why was the *Muller v. Oregon* case important? Why would protective legislation become controversial? (text, 750–751)

10. Why was the Triangle Fire so deadly? What were the consequences of this tragedy? Why and how did Frances Perkins get involved? (text, pp. 750–751; video segments 2, 3)

11. How did the theories of "reform Darwinism," pragmatism, and social engineering support the activism of the progressives? (text, p. 754)

12. How and why did Tom Johnson, Robert M. LaFollette, Hiram Johnson, and other local and state politicians further progressive reform? Who benefited from their efforts? What were the limits on local and state reform? (text, pp. 755–756; video segments 2, 3)

13. Why and how did President Theodore Roosevelt use antitrust suits to control the power of big business? What were the consequences of Roosevelt's actions regarding trusts? (text, pp. 756–758; video segment 4)

14. How did President Roosevelt handle the coal strike of 1902? How did he and his administration deal with railroad regulation? What did the term "Square Deal" mean? (text, pp. 758–760; video segment 4)

15. Who were the muckrakers? How did Jacob Riis expose urban living conditions and influence reform? How did Upton Sinclair's *The Jungle* help shape progressive reform? Why was the Pure Food and Drug Act important? (text, pp. 760–763; video segment 4)

16. What factors shaped President Roosevelt's approach to conservation issues? How did Gifford Pinchot and John Muir influence his views and actions? How and why did Roosevelt's policies regarding natural resources have lasting repercussions? (text, pp. 761, 764–767; video segment 4)

17. Why did President William Howard Taft have such a "troubled" presidency? (text, pp. 769–771)

18. How and why did the presidential election of 1912 reflect progressivism? Who were the candidates? What were their positions? What were the results? What was important about the election? (text, pp. 771–773)

19. What significant progressive reforms took place during the Woodrow Wilson administrations regarding tariffs, banking, and business regulation? What was important about the 16th and 17th Amendments? (text, pp. 773–775; video segment 4)

20. How did the progressives deal with child labor issues? What obstacles did they face in trying to bring about reform in this area? (text, p. 775)

21. What were the "radical" alternatives to progressivism in the early twentieth century? What success did Eugene Debs and the socialists have? What did the Industrial Workers of the World attempt to do at this time? (text, pp. 776–778)

22. How and why were women able to gain passage of the 19th Amendment during the progressive era? Why had this been so difficult? Why and how did progressives actually limit freedom and equality for African Americans and Asians? (text, pp. 778–782)

23. In summary, how and why did the progressives and their reforms transform America? What were the limits of progressivism? What was the legacy of progressive reform? (text, all pages; video segments 1–5)

HISTORICAL EXPERTS INTERVIEWED

Karl Brooks, Assistant Professor of History, University of Kansas, Lawrence, KS
Clayborne Carson, Professor of History and Editor of Martin Luther King, Jr. Papers, Stanford University, Stanford, CA
Eric Foner, Professor of History, Columbia University, New York, NY
David Gutierrez, Professor of History, University of California, San Diego, CA
Alice Kessler-Harris, Professor of History, Columbia University, New York, NY
David Levering Lewis, Julius Silver University Professor of History, New York University, New York, NY
Patricia Limerick, Faculty Director, Center of the American West, University of Colorado, Boulder, CO
Michael McGerr, Professor of History, Indiana University, Bloomington, IN
Sarah Stage, Professor, Arizona State University, West Campus, Phoenix, AZ
David Von Drehle, Staff Writer, *The Washington Post*, Washington, DC

FEATURED FAMILY MEMBER INTERVIEWED

Bill Cecil, Jr., Asheville, NC

PRACTICE TEST

The following items will help you evaluate your understanding of this lesson. Use the Answer Key at the end of the lesson to check your answers or to locate material related to this lesson.

Multiple Choice: Choose the letter of the best answer.

1. By 1900, the meaning of American identity at home _____.
   A. included most ethnic and racial minorities
   B. excluded more people than previously
   C. had been clearly defined by the 15th Amendment
   D. assured equal rights for all citizens

2. Progressive reformers were primarily concerned with _____.
   A. making democratic capitalism work better
   B. desegregating the nation's schools
   C. providing tax cuts for the rich
   D. nationalizing banks and railroads

3. American women of the late nineteenth and early twentieth centuries found that the settlement house movement _____.
   A. did not allow them to act in unorthodox ways
   B. excluded those who were not Protestant
   C. was dominated by white males
   D. was a good place to use their talents to help society

4. Progressives launched the social purity movement to _____.
   A. regulate the food industry
   B. attack prostitution and other vices
   C. advocate the use of birth control among immigrants
   D. clean up corrupt urban politics

5. Progressives justified segregation on the grounds that it _____.
   A. assured equal rights for all citizens
   B. adhered to the wishes of W.E.B. DuBois
   C. preserved state control over voting rights
   D. provided for a more stable society

6. As a reform governor of California from 1911 to 1917, Hiram Johnson _____.
   A. introduced the direct primary and strengthened the state's railroad commission
   B. endorsed conservation and signed an employer's liability law
   C. supported the initiative, referendum, and recall
   D. vetoed both the direct primary and the recall

7. The Triangle Shirtwaist Company fire illustrated the _____.
   A. need for government regulation of working conditions
   B. benefits of a free market business climate
   C. management's provision for safety of workers
   D. lack of the need for unions in American society

8. Taken together, President Theodore Roosevelt's actions in the anthracite coal strike of 1902 and the dissolution of Northern Securities in 1904 demonstrated that the government _____.
   A. intended to act independently of big business
   B. was willing to make deals with big business to maintain a stable economy
   C. would continue to side with management in major labor disputes
   D. was virtually powerless to withstand lobbyists and other powerful business interests

9. The Federal Reserve Act of 1913 _____.
   A. had little effect on the U.S. economy
   B. was passed over President Wilson's veto
   C. was the most significant piece of domestic legislation in Wilson's presidency
   D. was designed to curb the economic power of the federal government

10. Progressive reform illustrates that _____.
    A. political change usually happens easily
    B. middle-class people have little power
    C. a more just society is impossible
    D. legislation makes a difference

Short Answer: Your answer should specifically address the points indicated in one or two paragraphs.

11. How had American identity, freedom, and equality changed by the late nineteenth century? What challenges existed in these areas in 1900?

12. Why and how were women so active in the progressive movement? Cite the work of two specific women reformers to support your answer.

13. How and why was conservation of resources a major accomplishment of the progressives?

14. In what ways was the progressive movement paradoxical?

Essay Question: Your response should be several paragraphs long. Your answer should elaborate on the points indicated in a manner that expresses understanding of the material.

15. How and why did the progressives and their reforms transform America? What were the limits of progressivism? What was the legacy of progressive reform?

ANSWER KEY

	Answer	Learning Objectives	Focus Points	References
1.	B	LO 1	FP 1	Video segment 1
2.	A	LO 2	FP 3	Text, pp. 745–747; video segment 2
3.	D	LO 2	FP 4	Text, pp. 745–749; video segment 2
4.	B	LO 3	FP 5	Text, pp. 747–749; video segment 2
5.	D	LO 2, 3	FP 6	Text, pp. 777–782; video segment
6.	C	LO 3	FP 12	Text, p. 756
7.	A	LO 3	FP 10	Text, pp. 750–751; video segment 3
8.	A	LO 4	FP 14	Text, pp. 758–760; video segment 4
9.	C	LO 4	FP 19	Text, pp. 773–775; video segment 4
10.	D	LO 5	FP 23	Text, p. 782; video segment 5

11. ....LO 1....................FP 1 .... Video segment 1
 - Consider what America stood for in the world.
 - Who was being excluded from being an "American" at home? Why?
 - What threatened greater freedom and equality?

12. ....LO 2....................FP 3 .... Text, pp. 745–747; video segment 2
 - Why would women be more satisfied by being engaged with reform?
 - What social issues particularly concerned women?
 - Consider Jane Addams, Margaret Sanger, Frances Perkins, and Florence Kelley

13. .... LO 4.....................FP 16.............................. Text, pp.761, 764–767; video segment 4
    - What was the attitude toward natural resources before the progressive era?
    - What role did Theodore Roosevelt, Gifford Pinchot, and John Muir play?
    - What was done to conserve and preserve resources? What is the legacy?

14. .... LO 3, 4, 5.............FP 23 .... Text, p. 782; video segments 2–5
    - What is the meaning of a paradox?
    - Consider social purity and birth control, segregation and social justice, radical and centrist, freedom and regulation.

15. .... LO 2-5 ....FP 23 .... Text, all pages; video segments 1–5
    - Consider who the progressives were and what they were trying to accomplish.
    - What major reforms took place at the local, state, and national levels?
    - What limited reform at each level? How did the progressives limit themselves?
    - What reforms from that time remain? How is the progressive spirit still with us?

ENRICHMENT IDEAS

These activities are not required unless your instructor assigns them. They are offered as suggestions to help you learn more about the material presented in this lesson.

1. Research the work that went on at Hull House. Then write a well-developed essay in which you describe those activities and assess what Hull House meant to the community and to the progressive reform movement.

2. You are a progressive in the early twentieth century. In a well-reasoned essay, identify three major domestic issues facing the nation and explain how you propose to address these issues through government action.

SUGGESTED READINGS/RESOURCES

See the "Bibliography" on pages 782–783 if you wish to examine other books and resources related to the material discussed in this lesson.

Lesson 9

A War to End All Wars

OVERVIEW

When Woodrow Wilson became president in 1913, he indicated his foreign policy would stress "human rights, national integrity, and opportunity." He believed the mission of the United States was to be the bearer of justice, morality, and democracy—not the big stick. Despite his lofty idealism, Wilson presided over military intervention both in the Americas and Europe.

World War I, known as the Great War at the time, began during the summer of 1914 and presented the greatest challenge to Wilson's missionary diplomacy. The United States pursued its traditional policy of neutrality until April 2, 1917, when President Wilson asked Congress to declare war. Idealistically, this would be a war "to make the world safe for democracy."

Fighting "a war to end all wars" brought about a mobilization of human and material resources that affected all Americans. At home, the pluralistic society rallied around the flag, while dissenters sometimes went to jail. Production demands opened up jobs, and minorities moved to fill them. Progressives managed the economy and pushed through reforms as "war measures." Overseas, American military forces may have entered the war late, but they made a crucial difference. Finally, at the eleventh hour of the eleventh day of the eleventh month – November 11, 1918, Germany signed an armistice based on President Wilson's Fourteen Points.

At war's end, both Wilson and the United States appeared to stand at the pinnacle of world power. Soon, however, disruptions at home and disillusionment with the war prevailed. Wilson left office a broken man with his dreams unfulfilled. Why had this happened? What did it all mean?

LESSON ASSIGNMENT

Text: Roark, et.al., *The American Promise*
- Chapter 22, "World War I: The Progressive Crusade at Home and Abroad," pp. 786–823

Video: "A War to End All Wars," from the series *Transforming America*

LEARNING OBJECTIVES

This lesson examines American foreign policy during the era of World War I, the effects of that war at home and abroad, and the legacy of the war. Upon the completion of this lesson, you should be able to:

1. Explain President Woodrow Wilson's approach to foreign policy.

2. Analyze the causes of World War I and the entry of the United States into that war.

3. Analyze the political, economic, and social effects of the war on the American home front.

4. Assess American military involvement in World War I and Wilson's attempts to shape the peace.

5. Assess the legacy of World War I and President Wilson.

LESSON FOCUS POINTS

The following questions are designed to help you get the most benefit from the sources selected for this lesson. For reference purposes, the video is divided into five segments: (1) Introduction, (2) "On the Fence," (3) "Crusade for Democracy," (4) "Over There," and (5) Summary Analysis: "Wilson's Ghost."

1. Upon entering office, how did President Woodrow Wilson approach foreign policy? How was he different from his predecessors? Why did he approve of intervention in Mexico and other Latin American countries? (text, pp. 787–790)

2. Why did a major war break out in Europe in 1914? Who was fighting whom? (text, pp. 790–791; video segment 1)

3. Why did the United States declare neutrality? What were the advantages of being neutral? Why and how did the U.S. neutrality favor the Allies? (text, pp. 791–792; video segment 2)

4. How was American neutrality violated? What was important about the sinking of the *Lusitania* and German submarine warfare in general? (text, p. 792–793; video segment 2)

5. Why did Germany declare unrestricted submarine warfare in early 1917? What was important about the Zimmermann Telegram? In the end, why did the United States enter the war on the side of the Allies? (text, pp. 793–794; video segment 2)

6. How did the United States increase the size of its armed forces? How were the recruits trained? Why was General John J. Pershing chosen to head the American Expeditionary Force? (text, pp. 787–788, 794–795; video segment 3)

7. How and why were American forces important in the Allied victory in the European war? What was the cost of war in terms of lives lost? (text, pp. 794–800; video segment 4)

8. What steps did the progressives take to manage the war mobilization at home? How did the war affect American workers? (text, pp. 800–802; video segment 3)

9. How and why was the passage of the 18th and 19th Amendments connected to the war effort? What was important about these amendments? (text, pp. 802–804, 806–807; video segment 3)

10. Generally, what did World War I mean for African Americans? Why did so many African Americans undertake a "great migration" at home during the war years? How were they received in the North? What was important about the "great migration?" (text, pp. 815, 818; viideo segment 3)

11. Why were there so many immigrants from Mexico entering the United States between 1910–1920? What were the results of this immigration? (text, pp. 818–819)

12. Why was the Committee on Public Information created? What did it do? How was anti-German sentiment expressed inside the United States? (text, pp. 804–805; video segment 3)

13. How were dissenters treated during the war? How could they express their opinions? What was important about the Espionage Act and the Sedition Act? (text, pp. 804–805; video segment 3)

14. How and why did President Wilson use the Fourteen Points to shape the peace? How did the Allied leaders view Wilson and his idealism? (text, pp. 805, 808–810; video segment 4)

15. What were the main points of the Treaty of Versailles? Why were many disappointed with it? (text, pp. 809–810; video segment 4)

16. Why did President Wilson fail to gain the Senate's ratification of the Treaty of Versailles? Why was joining the League of Nations so controversial? Why was the failure of the United States to join the League important? (text, 810–811; video segment 4)

17. Why was there so much economic hardship and labor upheaval immediately after the war? How was this expressed? (text, pp. 811–813)

18. Why was there a "Red Scare" during 1919–1920? What happened during this period of fear? Why did the "Red Scare" end? What were its lingering effects? (text, pp. 813–814, 816–817)

19. What were the results of the 1920 presidential election? What did Warren Harding's victory indicate? (text, pp. 819–820)

20. In summary, how and why did the United States enter and participate in World War I? What was the legacy of the war and of Woodrow Wilson? (text, all pages; video, segments 2–5)

HISTORICAL EXPERTS INTERVIEWED

Eric Arnesen, Professor of History and African American Studies, University of Illinois, Chicago, IL
Calvin L. Christman, Professor, Cedar Valley College, Lancaster, TX
Fraser Harbutt, Associate Professor, Emory University, Atlanta, GA
George Herring, Professor of History, University of Kentucky, Lexington, KY
David Levering Lewis, Julius Silver University Professor of History, New York University, New York, NY
Sarah Stage, Professor, Arizona State University, West Campus, Phoenix, AZ

PRACTICE TEST

The following items will help you evaluate your understanding of this lesson. Use the Answer Key at the end of the lesson to check your answers or to locate material related to this lesson.

Multiple Choice: Choose the letter of the best answer.

1. President Wilson's foreign policy was based on _____.
   A. the "big stick" in Latin America
   B. dollar diplomacy around the world
   C. an Open Door with China
   D. his belief in moral duties

2. The assassination of Archduke Ferdinand in 1914 led to a war in Europe because _____.
   A. anarchists were in control of Austria
   B. of military, economic, and political rivalries
   C. his assassin was a German nationalist
   D. communism dominated politics on the continent

3. In exchange for its neutrality in World War I, the United States insisted on _____.
   A. its right to offer nonmilitary aid to the Allies
   B. free trade with all nations at war
   C. an embargo on all private passenger ships
   D. a role in the peace process

4. After the Germans sank the *Lusitania*, President Wilson _____.
   A. threatened a break in diplomatic relations with Germany
   B. followed the advice of William Jennings Bryan
   C. declared war on Germany
   D. warned Americans about sailing on foreign ships

5. The immediate cause of President Wilson's decision to ask Congress for a declaration of war against Germany in 1917 was _____.
   A. the Zimmermann telegram to Mexico
   B. German submarine attacks on American vessels in the sea lanes to Great Britain
   C. pressure from Theodore Roosevelt and other interventionists
   D. the discovery of German submarines off the Atlantic coast

6. Progressive management of World War I at home was illustrated by all of the following EXCEPT _____.
   A. bureaucrats administered to special needs
   B. government was a major player
   C. businesses were all nationalized
   D. labor made some gains

7. The Committee on Public Information was created by President Wilson to _____.
   A. encourage the public to watch for German spies
   B. ban novels written by German authors
   C. stir up patriotism through posters, pamphlets, cartoons, and press releases
   D. quiet critics like Jane Addams and Emily Greene Balch

8. Arrival of American troops on the front lines in 1918 was critical because they provided all of the following EXCEPT _____.
   A. manpower needed for the Allies
   B. a morale boost for discouraged Allied troops
   C. messages demanding unconditional surrender
   D. momentum to turn the tide on the battlefields

9. The Versailles Treaty was a bitter disappointment to President Wilson's supporters, but his Fourteen Points were honored in the inclusion of _____.
   A. the League of Nations
   B. freedom of the seas
   C. self-determination for Germany's colonies in Asia
   D. war reparations to be paid by Germany

10. The Red Scare of 1919 and 1920 was a _____.
    A. reaction in the United States to the demobilization of the army
    B. series of strikes led by Communist radicals
    C. reaction to labor unrest, Russian Bolshevism, and terrorist attacks
    D. protest by socialist reformers who marched in Washington

Short Answer: Your answer should specifically address the points indicated in one or two paragraphs.

11. Why did the United States enter World War I on the side of the Allies?

12. How did World War I affect the status of women, African Americans, and people of Mexican descent in America?

13. Why did the Senate refuse to ratify the Treaty of Versailles? What was important about that decision?

Essay Question: Your response should be several paragraphs long. Your answer should elaborate on the points indicated in a manner that expresses understanding of the material.

14. How and why did the United States participate in World War I? What was the legacy of American involvement and of Woodrow Wilson's diplomacy?

ANSWER KEY

	Answer	Learning Objectives	Focus Points	References
1.	D	LO 1	FP 1	Text, pp. 787–790
2.	B	LO 2	FP 2	Text, pp. 790–791; video segment 1
3.	B	LO 2	FP 3	Text, pp. 791–792
4.	A	LO 2	FP 4	Text, pp. 792–793; video segment 2
5.	B	LO 2	FP 5	Text, pp. 793–794; video segment 2
6.	C	LO 3	FP 8	Text, pp. 800–802; video segment 4
7.	C	LO 3	FP 12	Text, pp. 804–805; video segment 3
8.	C	LO 4	FP 7	Text, pp. 794–800; video segment 4
9.	A	LO 4	FP 15	Text, pp. 809–810; video segment 4
10.	C	LO 5	FP 18	Text, pp. 813–814, 816–817

11. .... LO 2 .... FP 5 .... Text, pp. 793–794; video segment 2
   - Consider the influence of economic and cultural connections.
   - What actions by Germany justified war?
   - How did U.S. political objectives mesh with those of the Allies?

12. .... LO 3 .... FP 9, 10, 11 .... Text, pp. 802–804, 806–807, 815, 818–819; video segment 3
   - What rights did women gain? What opportunities were available?
   - Consider the "great migration" and African American participation.
   - Why were so many Mexicans migrating to the United States? What conditions were they facing?

13. ....LO 4, 5.................FP 16...................................Text, pp. 810–811; video segments 4–5
    - Consider the roles of personality, partisanship, and principle in the Senate.
    - Why was President Wilson unwilling to compromise?
    - What did the decision indicate about America? What effect did the U.S. decision have on the League of Nations and its effectiveness?

14. ....LO 5.....................FP 20....................................... Text, all pages; video segments 2–5
    - Consider the factors that led the United States to enter the war.
    - What role did American armed forces play? How were soldiers affected?
    - How was the wartime mobilization managed at home? How were people affected?
    - What significant changes took place for minorities?
    - How did Wilson help shape the peace?
    - What was important about the Senate's refusal to ratify the Treaty of Versailles?
    - How is "Wilson's Ghost" still visible today?

ENRICHMENT IDEAS

These activities are not required unless your instructor assigns them. They are offered as suggestions to help you learn more about the material presented in this lesson.

1. Read the "Documenting the American Promise" segment of the text on "The Final Push for Woman Suffrage" (pp. 806–808). Then submit a well-developed essay in which you answer the questions posed in the text.

2. You are a U.S. Senator in 1919–1920. Write a position paper in which you thoughtfully and thoroughly explain your vote for OR against the ratification of the Treaty of Versailles.

SUGGESTED READINGS/RESOURCES

See the "Bibliography" on page 821 of the text if you wish to examine other books and resources related to the material discussed in this lesson.

Lesson 10

Modern Times

OVERVIEW

Historian Jeffrey Moran remarks in the video for this lesson that he sees "the 1920s as the first recognizably modern decade" in American history. Automobiles rolled off the assembly line and became a major driver in American economic and social life. Americans heard their first commercial radio broadcast in 1920, and by the end of the decade forty percent of homes had radios. Advertisers spurred sales of the latest home appliances and broadened the consumer culture. Some corporate managers initiated a system of "welfare capitalism" to improve the work environment and provide more leisure time for employees. People enjoyed movies and spectator sports, both of which created celebrities and business opportunities. The stock market took off to unprecedented heights. The business of America was business, and the government rolled back progressive measures enacted a decade earlier. Herbert Hoover, elected president in 1928, predicted the abolition of poverty. Of course, millions of Americans were poor, especially farmers and large numbers of minorities.

While the economy seemed to be ushering in a new era of prosperity, Americans were dazzled and sometimes troubled by cultural transitions. New values appeared to replace the old, as flapper girls danced the Charleston, smoked cigarettes, and sipped on illegal booze. More serious-minded feminists were talking about an equal rights amendment and birth control. Organized crime captured headlines in big-city newspapers, and Hollywood stars captured the hearts and imaginations of those infatuated with the lives of the rich and famous. Changing times and attitudes provided settings for enduring literature, music, and art, including a flowering of black artistic expression related to the Harlem Renaissance.

Those on the conservative side of the cultural clash responded with a series of attempts to maintain what they considered to be the true American values. The anarchist immigrants Sacco and Vanzetti, arrested during the postwar Red Scare in 1920, were executed in 1927. Protestant fundamentalists tried to hold the line against scientific theories espoused by educators like John Scopes. A resurgent Ku Klux Klan targeted those they defined as less than "100 percent American" with a new round of domestic terror. Nativist fears were strong enough to bring about a significant change in American immigration policy.

Indeed, modern times were upon us. And Americans then, as now, had to deal with the consequences.

LESSON ASSIGNMENT

Text: Roark, et. al., *The American Promise*
- Chapter 23, "From New Era to Great Depression," pp. 824–849

Video: "Modern Times," from the series *Transforming America*

LEARNING OBJECTIVES

This lesson examines the political, economic, social, and cultural transitions and tensions characteristic of the 1920s. Upon completing this lesson, you should be able to:

1. Analyze the changing nature of the American economy and the extent of prosperity in the 1920s.

2. Assess the political leadership of the era.

3. Describe the major cultural developments occurring in the 1920s.

4. Analyze the reaction to the social and cultural changes.

5. Assess the significance of the developments of the 1920s in shaping a modern America.

LESSON FOCUS POINTS

The following questions are designed to help you get the most benefit from the sources selected for this lesson. For reference purposes, the video is divided into five segments: (1) Introduction, (2) "The Business of America is Business," (3) "The Old Radio Won't Do," (4) "The Tribal Twenties," and (5) Summary Analysis: "The America We Recognize."

1. How and why did the Republican administrations of the 1920s support business? How did the Supreme Court show its partiality to business management? (text, pp. 826–828; video segment 2)

2. How and why did the automobile become such a driving force in the American economy in the 1920s? (text, pp. 824–826, 829–831; video segment 2)

3. Why was Henry Ford so central to the new wave of industrialism? What was the meaning of "Fordism?" (text, pp. 824–826; video segment 2)

4. What is "welfare capitalism?" Why and how was this practiced in the 1920s? (text, p. 830; video segment 2)

5. Who benefited most and least from the economic expansion of the 1920s? Why was this the case? (text, pp. 830–831; video segment 2)

6. What roles did the radio play in the social and cultural lives of Americans during the 1920s? (video segment 3)

7. How and why did a new consumer culture develop in the 1920s? What were the characteristics of this consumer culture? (text, pp. 830–834; video segment 3)

8. Why did national prohibition go into effect in the 1920s? What were the costs and benefits of national prohibition? Was prohibition a bad idea? How does the prohibition of alcohol compare to the more recent prohibition of drugs? (text, pp. 835–836)

9. To what degree was there "a new woman" emerging during the 1920s? How were the political, social, and economic conditions of women changing? (text, pp. 836–840; video segment 3)

10. To what extent did a "new Negro" emerge in the 1920s? What did this mean? Why did this happen? What is the importance of Marcus Garvey? (text, pp. 840–843)

11. What is the Harlem Renaissance? Who are the artists, writers, and musicians associated with it? What is the significance of the Harlem Renaissance? (text, pp. 840–841; video segment 4)

12. How and why did the proliferation of movies, music, sports, as well as radios, shape a national culture at this time? (text, pp. 841, 844)

13. Why did this era produce a "lost generation" of American writers? Who is associated with this period of literature? What characterized this literature? (text, p. 845)

14. Why did rural Americans lead the resistance to cultural changes taking place in the 1920s? (text, pp. 845–849)

15. Examine Map 23.2 on page 846 of the textbook. What does the map tell you about demographic changes in the 1920s? (text, p. 846)

16. What did the trial, imprisonment, and execution of Nicola Sacco and Bartolomeo Vanzetti illustrate about the 1920s? (text, p. 847; video segments 1 and 5)

17. Why was there so much nativist and "anti-radical" sentiment in the 1920s? How did the Immigration Act of 1924 (Johnson-Reid National Origins Act) reflect fears and bigotry? What was the significance of this act? (text, pp. 845–847; video segment 4)

18. Why did the Ku Klux Klan have such a large following in the early 1920s? How did Klan members terrorize their victims? Why did the Klan fall into public disfavor? (text, pp. 847–848)

19. Why and how did the Scopes Trial illustrate the cultural tensions of the 1920s? What was the outcome of the trial? (text, pp. 848–849; video segment 4)

20. How did the 1928 presidential election reflect most of the significant developments of the 1920s? Who won the election? Why? (text, p. 849)

21. In summary, how and why was America transformed during the 1920s? How did the developments of that era reflect a modern America? (text, all pages; video segments 1–5)

HISTORICAL EXPERTS INTERVIEWED

Pamela Laird, Associate Professor, University of Colorado, Denver, CO
David Levering Lewis, Julius Silver University Professor of History, New York University, New York, NY
Lisa McGirr, Dunwalke Associate Professor, Harvard University, Cambridge, MA
Jeffrey Moran, Department Chair and Professor of History, University of Kansas, Lawrence, KS
Susan Strasser, Professor of History, University of Delaware, Newark, DE

PRACTICE TEST

The following items will help you evaluate your understanding of this lesson. Use the Answer Key at the end of the lesson to check your answers or to locate material related to each question.

Multiple Choice: Choose the letter of the best answer.

1. In general, the 1920s can be characterized as a period in which _____.
   A. economic depression affected the majority of the American people
   B. progressive reform reached its climax
   C. new values clashed with old values
   D. little technological progress occurred

2. The Republican administrations of the 1920s believed that _____.
   A. free trade would promote prosperity
   B. the rich should be taxed more aggressively
   C. business regulation should be kept to a minimum
   D. farmers should be given price supports for their crops

3. "Fordism" implies all of the following EXCEPT _____.
   A. auto workers are better off with strong union representation
   B. mass production of identical items
   C. monotonous work on the moving assembly line
   D. workers should make enough money to be consumers

4. One key element in the expansion of the consumer culture in the 1920s was _____.
   A. commercial advertising on radio broadcasts
   B. the success of bootleggers in supplying alcoholic beverages
   C. a sharp increase in the immigrant population
   D. the availability of cheap products imported from Asia

5. The Harlem Renaissance is a term that refers to _____.
   A. white American writers who fled to Europe during the 1920s
   B. black American intellectuals and artists who stressed self-confidence
   C. residential rebuilding efforts in northern Manhattan
   D. the success of the NAACP in overturning segregation laws

6. The National Origins Immigration Act of 1924 (Johnson-Reid) had the effect of _____.
   A. restricting the number and type of immigrants who could enter America
   B. abolishing the Chinese Exclusion Act
   C. acknowledging the contributions of southeastern Europeans
   D. supporting the inscription on the Statue of Liberty

7. The Ku Klux Klan gained support in the 1920s because of _____.
   A. financial backing from leading industrialists
   B. reaction to immigration and urbanization
   C. lack of moral values in the American people
   D. indifferent attitudes toward law enforcement

8. The trial and eventual execution of Sacco and Vanzetti symbolized _____.
   A. a triumph for the justice of the American judicial system
   B. the anti-foreign hysteria of much of the 1920s
   C. a unity of sentiment in America regarding radicals
   D. the power of radio to shape public opinion

9. The Scopes Trial ended with _____.
   A. reassurance that academic freedom would be respected
   B. William Jennings Bryan finally winning a significant victory
   C. fundamentalism losing significant influence in the South
   D. deep divisions still apparent between rural and urban America

10. Herbert Hoover won the presidential election of 1928 for all of the following reasons EXCEPT _____.
    A. Republican control of inner city voters
    B. perceptions of his leadership ability
    C. prosperity making voters reluctant to change parties
    D. optimism that good times would continue

Short-Answer: Your answer should be one or two paragraphs long and specifically address the points indicated.

11. What was Calvin Coolidge's philosophy of government? How was this philosophy expressed during his administration?

12. How did the radio transform America during the 1920s? Cite two specific examples in your answer.

13. What were the costs and benefits of national prohibition? What is the connection of prohibition to contemporary drug laws?

14. To what extent was there a "new woman" emerging during the 1920s? Explain briefly.

Essay Question: Your answer should be several paragraphs long and express a clear understanding of the points indicated.

15. How and why was America transformed during the 1920s? How did the developments of that era reflect a modern America? Use four specific examples to substantiate your answer.

ANSWER KEY

Answer	Learning Objectives	Focus Points	References
1. C	LO 5	FP 21	Text, all pages; video segments 1–5
2. C	LO 2	FP 1	Text, pp. 826–828; video segment 2
3. A	LO 1	FP 3	video segment 2
4. A	LO 1	FP 6, 7	Text, pp. 830–834; video segment 3
5. B	LO 3	FP 11	Text, pp. 840–841; video segment 4
6. A	LO 4	FP 17	Text, pp. 845–847; video segment 4
7. B	LO 4	FP 18	Text, pp. 847–848; video segment 4
8. B	LO 4	FP 16	Text, p. 847; video segments 1, 5
9. D	LO 4	FP 19	Text, pp. 848–849; video segment 4
10. A	LO 4	FP 20	Text, p. 849

11. ....LO 2................FP 1..............................Text, pp. 827–828; video segment 2
    - Consider Coolidge's statement, "the business of America is business."
    - What steps were taken to reduce government regulation?
    - How did tax cuts illustrate Coolidge's philosophy?

12. ....LO 1, 3..............FP 6, 7.......................Text, pp. 830–834; video segments 3, 4
    - Consider the business/consumer aspects of buying and selling radios.
    - How did radio affect advertising?
    - What were the social effects of radio on mass culture?

13. ....LO 4................FP 8..Text, pp. 835–836
    - What effect did prohibition have on the consumption of alcohol?
    - What was the cost of rather widespread violations of the law?
    - How are drug laws similar to and different from prohibition?

14. ....LO 3................FP 9............................Text, pp. 836–840; video segment 3
    - Consider the images and realities of women in the 1920s.
    - How did the new political status of women play out?
    - What economic changes were taking place?
    - What options did women have? What limited the options?

15. .... LO 5 .... FP 21 .... Text, all pages; all video segments
    - What demographic information indicated a move toward modern America?
    - Consider the major business and consumer developments.
    - How did the lives of women and minorities change?
    - What were the major social and cultural changes? How were social norms changing?
    - How did traditionalists react to change? What steps did they take?
    - Connect the 1920s to the society you see around you.

ENRICHMENT IDEAS

These activities are not required unless your instructor assigns them. They are offered as suggestions to help you learn more about the material presented in this lesson.

1. What does the image on page 831 of the text say about America in 1929? Refer to the publisher's website and complete the visual activity indicated.

2. Research the activities of the Ku Klux Klan in the 1920s in your area. In a well-developed report, describe your findings. (Cite your sources in your report.)

3. In a well-developed essay, examine why the National Origins Act was a turning point in American immigration history. What is different about immigration laws today? How do immigration laws help transform American identity?

4. In a well-developed essay, compare and contrast Marcus Garvey's approach to issues confronting African Americans in the 1920s to the approaches W.E.B. DuBois and Booker T. Washington had already articulated. What was the importance of Garvey's position?

SUGGESTED READINGS/RESOURCES

See the "Bibliography" on pages 858–859 of the textbook if you wish to examine other books and resources related to the material presented in this lesson.

Lesson 11

The Great Depression

OVERVIEW

The Great Depression of the 1930s was one of the most defining experiences in American history. It clearly separated the generation that lived through it from the ones that lived before and after. Besides the economic troubles, the American people who experienced those hard times carried with them "invisible scars" for the rest of their lives. Why did the Great Depression occur? How did people cope? How did the experience transform America?

The Great Depression was much more than the stock market crash of late 1929, which is associated with the beginning of the era. The crash would not have led to a depression if there had not been serious problems throughout the economy: weak corporate and banking structures, a distorted distribution of income, international economic troubles, and poor political and economic leadership.

As the depressing times persisted, people had to cope as best they could. Self-help was in vogue, and they helped each other. They sought escape through movies, songs, and inexpensive social gatherings. However, most family relationships were strained, and many men left home. Minorities became convenient targets for frustrated majorities. Corporations abandoned their "welfare capitalism" schemes of the 1920s. There was no national welfare system at the time, and private charities and state efforts at relief could not meet the needs of the poor. Meanwhile, President Herbert Hoover could not bring himself to support direct federal relief.

By 1932, the American economy had collapsed. Protests in rural America, Detroit, and Washington, D.C., had turned violent. The greatest national crisis since the Civil War was at hand, and the American people were desperately looking for new leadership.

LESSON ASSIGNMENT

Text: Roark, et.al., *The American Promise*
- Chapter 23, "From New Era to Great Depression," pp. 850–861
- Chapter 24, "The New Deal Experiment," pp. 863–865

Video: "The Great Depression," from the series *Transforming America*

LEARNING OBJECTIVES

This lesson examines the causes and consequences of the Great Depression. Upon completion of this lesson, you should be able to:

1. Explain the causes of the Great Crash and the Great Depression.

2. Describe how the American people coped with the hardships of the Depression.

3. Analyze how President Hoover and his administration responded to the crisis.

4. Analyze the consequences of the Great Depression.

LESSON FOCUS POINTS

The following questions are designed to help you get the most benefit from the sources selected for this lesson. For reference purposes, the video is divided into five segments: (1) Introduction, (2) "When Capitalism Failed," (3) "Hard Time Blues," (4) "Something is Radically Wrong," and (5) Summary Analysis: "Stormy Weather."

1. What role does the stock market play in capitalism? Why did the stock market crash in October 1929? Why did the crash trigger a depression? (text, pp. 851–852; video segment 2)

2. Why and how was this depression different from those that had occurred before? (video segment 2)

3. Why did so many banks fail at this time? How did this affect depositors? (text, p. 851; video segment 2)

4. Why was there a poor distribution of wealth and income in the 1920s? What effects did this have on the economy? (text, p. 851; video segment 2)

5. What problems were present in the international economy? Why did trade policies make the situation worse? (text, p. 851; video segment 2)

6. How and why did President Hoover deal with the economic collapse as he did? What steps did he take? How did he continue the trickle-down economics of his immediate predecessors? What limited Hoover's actions? (text, pp. 850–853; video segment 2)

7. Generally, how did the American people cope with the hardships of the depression? How were men, women, children, and families affected? (text, pp. 853–855; video segment 3)

8. In particular, how were African Americans and Mexican Americans affected by the depression? (text, pp. 855–857; video segment 3)

9. Why did so many people blame themselves for their economic depression? How did this affect their reactions to their plight? (text, pp. 853–858; video segment 3)

10. Why and how did President Hoover eventually become an object of ridicule? (text, p. 856; video segment 4)

11. How did movies deal with the depression? Why were they a popular escape from the hard times? Why did the public express some tolerance for outlaws? (text, p. 856; video segment 1)

12. Why did unemployed workers march on the Ford Motor Company in March, 1932? What were the results of this protest? (text, p. 856; video segment 4)

13. How and why were farmers and farm workers protesting? What effect did their protests have? (text, pp. 856–857; video segment 4)

14. Why were socialists and communists gaining support in America in the 1930s? How and why did the Harlan County Coal Strike and the case of the "Scottsboro Boys" win adherents for their view? (text, pp. 857–858; video segment 4)

15. Why did World War I veterans march on Washington in 1932? Why and how were the Bonus Marchers driven out of the capital city? What were the results of this action? (text, pp. 863–865; video segment 4)

16. In summary, why did the Great Depression happen? How did people cope? How did the Great Depression change America? (text, all pages; video segments 1–5)

HISTORICAL EXPERTS INTERVIEWED

Michael Bernstein, Professor of History, University of California, San Diego, CA
Kevin Boyle, Associate Professor, Ohio State University, Columbus, OH
Joan Hoff, Research Professor of History, Montana State University, Bozeman, MT
David Kennedy, Professor of History, Stanford University, Stanford, CA
Nelson Lichtenstein, Professor of History, University of California, Santa Barbara, CA
Guadelupe San Miquel, Jr., Professor of History, University of Houston, Houston, TX

FEATURED FAMILY MEMBERS INTERVIEWED

Edward Archuleta, Santa Fe, NM
Vine Deloria, Jr., Golden, CO
Harry Dingenthal, Garland, TX
Eddie Fung, Santa Cruz, CA
Charlene McAden, Blooming Grove, TX
Bill Neebe, Wilmette, IL
Judy Yung, Santa Cruz, CA

PRACTICE TEST

The following items will help you evaluate your understanding of this lesson. Use the Answer Key at the end of the lesson to check your answers or to locate material related to each question.

Multiple Choice: Choose the letter of the best answer.

1. When Herbert Hoover moved into the White House in 1929, the U.S. economy was marked by _____.
   A. a huge disparity in wealth between rich and poor
   B. low tariffs and a strong balance of trade with foreign nations
   C. a narrowing of the gap between rich and poor
   D. a reluctance among consumers to buy on credit

2. One of the biggest weaknesses of the stock market in the 1920s was _____.
   A. poor oversight by the Securities and Exchange Commission
   B. over extension of credit
   C. lack of new investment opportunities
   D. interest rates were too high

3. On the international level, the Great Depression deepened when the _____.
   A. communists took over in Russia
   B. United States forgave World War I debts
   C. industrial nations raised protective tariffs
   D. League of Nations collapsed

4. As the United States slipped into the Great Depression in the early 1930s, President Hoover's most generous response was to lend government funds to _____.
   A. the millions of Americans who had lost their jobs
   B. rural black Southerners who had been in an agricultural depression for years
   C. American banks, insurance companies, and railroads
   D. faltering West Coast shippers plying the Pacific trade

5. Those hardest hit by the Great Depression were _____.
   A. bankers and other business people
   B. union members
   C. western miners and cattle ranchers
   D. the unemployed, tenant farmers, and sharecroppers

6. In the video, "The Great Depression," Professor David Kennedy observes that the tendency of Americans in the 1930s to blame themselves for the depression illustrates the _____.
   A. dark underside of the American value of individualism
   B. resiliency of the American character
   C. effectiveness of corporate propaganda
   D. futility of direct federal relief programs

7. The outcome of a protest by three thousand farmers who dumped thousands of gallons of milk into ditches during the Great Depression was _____.
   A. a shortage of milk that forced Congress to guarantee farm prices
   B. a bloody confrontation with the National Guard
   C. an increase in the public's awareness of farmers' grievances
   D. anger that the farmers would waste food while people were starving

8. During the Great Depression, _____.
   A. radical groups were discredited
   B. the old corporate elites proved capable of solving the problems
   C. local and state governments met all relief needs
   D. socialist and communist groups attracted more American members

Short Answer: Your answer should specifically address the points indicated in one or two paragraphs.

9. Why and how did people blame President Herbert Hoover for the Great Depression?

10. Why did a poor distribution of income develop in the 1920s? Why did this condition help cause the Great Depression?

Essay Question: Your response should be several paragraphs long and should elaborate on the points indicated in a manner that expresses understanding of the material.

11. Explain the major causes of the Great Depression. How did people cope with the economic crisis? How did the Great Depression transform America?

ANSWER KEY

	Answer	Learning Objectives	Focus Points	References
1.	A	LO 1	FP 4	Text, p. 851; video segment 2
2.	B	LO 1	FP 1	Text, pp. 851–852; video segment 2
3.	C	LO 1	FP 5	Text, p. 851; video segment 2
4.	C	LO 3	FP 6	Text, p. 853; video segment 2
5.	D	LO 2	FP 7	Text, pp. 853–855; video segment 3
6.	A	LO 2	FP 9	Video segment 3
7.	C	LO 2	FP 13	Text, pp. 856–857; video segment 4
8.	D	LO 4	FP 14	Text, pp. 857–858; video segment 4
9.		LO 3	FP 6, 10	Text, pp. 850–853, 856; video segments 2, 4

- Consider Hoover's personality and political philosophy.
- Why did he appear to be callous toward the poor?
- How did people ridicule him?

10. .... LO 1 .... FP 4 .... Text, p. 851; video segment 2
    - What sectors of the economy were hurting in the 1920s?
    - How did trickle-down economics affect income distribution?
    - What happens to consumption when income is poorly distributed?
    - What is the result of lower consumption?

11. .... LO 1–4 .... FP 16 .... Text, all pages; video segments 1–5
    - Consider problems in the stock market, banking, income distribution, international economy, and economic and political leadership.
    - What did people do to survive? Who did they blame?
    - What effects did the depression have on attitudes toward old elites and the role of the federal government?

ENRICHMENT IDEAS

These activities are not required unless your instructor assigns them. They are offered as suggestions to help you learn more about the material presented in this lesson.

1. There are still people alive who clearly remember the Great Depression. Interview some of these folks, preferably family members, about their experiences. Try to determine how the Great Depression changed their lives and the lives of their descendants. After the interviews, write a report in which you describe your own conclusions regarding the effects of the Great Depression and how people coped.

2. Research the effects of the Great Depression on the community in which you live. Then submit a report in which you describe your findings.

3. Read the book *Hard Times* by Studs Terkel. Then write a review of the book. Include in your review five specific examples of personal stories that you found particularly interesting.

SUGGESTED READINGS/RESOURCES

See the "Bibliography" on pages 858–859 and 899 of the text if you wish to examine other books and resources related to the material discussed in this lesson.

Lesson 12

A New Deal

OVERVIEW

While campaigning for president in 1932, Franklin D. Roosevelt offered "a new deal" for the American people. Once elected, FDR proceeded to implement a series of reforms that fundamentally reshaped America. While the New Deal did not bring full economic recovery, it did provide an unprecedented degree of security to national institutions and to millions of people previously left on the fringes of the American promise. How and why had this happened? What were the limits of the New Deal? What is its legacy?

FDR approached the presidency and the crisis of the Great Depression without fear. He had a vision "to make a country in which no one is left out." He exuded confidence that he could make things happen. He was willing to experiment, and he communicated with the American people. He stands with Abraham Lincoln as a catalyst in transforming America.

Critics of FDR maintain that he and his New Deal reforms either went too far or not far enough. At the time these reforms were being enacted, essentially during a five-year period between 1933 and 1938, the future of democratic capitalism may have been in the balance. Financial institutions, businesses, farmers, laborers, minorities – in short, Americans and the nation they lived in experienced fundamental change. Relationships, especially between the American people and their government, would never again be the same.

LESSON ASSIGNMENT

Text: Roark, et. al., *The American Promise*
- Chapter 24, "The New Deal Experiment," pp. 862–901

Video: "A New Deal," from the series *Transforming America*

LEARNING OBJECTIVES

This lesson examines the importance of President Franklin D. Roosevelt and the New Deal in transforming America. Upon completion of this lesson, you should be able to:

1. Explain the initial responses of Franklin D. Roosevelt and the New Deal to the crisis of the Great Depression.

2. Explain the evolution of New Deal policies, especially those affecting business, the unemployed, laborers, farmers, and minorities.

3. Analyze the effects of FDR and the New Deal on the presidency and American politics.

4. Assess the short- and long-term consequences of New Deal reforms.

LESSON FOCUS POINTS

The following questions are designed to help you get the most benefit from the sources selected for this lesson. For reference purposes, the video is divided into five segments: (1) Introduction, (2) "A Direct Connection," (3) "Making Life More Secure," (4) "The New Deal Coalition," and (5) Summary Analysis: "A Big Deal."

1. What personal and political experiences helped shape Franklin D. Roosevelt before he became president? Why did he win the presidential election of 1932? (text, pp. 865–868)

2. What were FDR's most effective qualities as a political leader? Who were his major advisers? (text, pp. 868–869; video introduction, segment 1)

3. What was the priority agenda of FDR and the New Dealers? What ideas guided their actions? (text, pp. 868–869, 872; video segment 1)

4. How did the New Deal reform banking and financial markets? What were the effects of these actions? (text, pp. 872–873; video introduction)

5. What relief programs were initiated under the New Deal? What conservation programs were undertaken? How did these efforts affect the American people? (text, pp. 873–875; video introduction, segment 1)

6. How did the New Deal transform American agriculture? (text, pp. 875–876, 880–883; video introduction)

7. What was the rationale behind the National Industrial Recovery Act? What were its main provisions? Why did the NRA have limited success? (text, pp. 876–879)

8. To what extent had the New Deal's first "Hundred Days" provided relief, recovery, and reform? (text, pp. 868–877; video introduction, segment 1)

9. What groups resisted business reform? Why did they do so? (text, pp. 877–880)

10. Who benefited from the New Deal's agricultural policies? Who lost out? What was the Dust Bowl? Who were the "Okies?" (text, pp. 880–882)

11. How and why did Upton Sinclair, Charles Coughlin, Francis Townsend, and Huey Long challenge the New Deal? What effect did they have? (text, pp. 882–884)

12. Why did FDR and the New Dealers move the United States toward a "welfare state" after 1935? What did that mean? How did the WPA provide public welfare? (text, pp. 884–886)

13. What were the main provisions of the Wagner Act? Why was this legislation so important? (text, pp. 886–888; video segment 2)

14. Why and how did the CIO emerge in the mid-1930s? What was important about the CIO? What was the significance of the "sit-down" strike against General Motors in 1937? (text, pp. 886–888; video segment 2)

15. Why was the Fair Labor Standards Act important? What did it accomplish? What were its limits? (text, pp. 896, 898; video segment 2)

16. What were the main provisions of the Social Security Act of 1935? Why was this legislation controversial? Why was it so important? (text, pp. 888–889; video segment 3)

17. How did Frances Perkins influence and symbolize the New Deal's commitment to labor reform? (text, p. 869; video segment 3)

18. How and why did the New Deal have mixed results for African Americans, Hispanic Americans, Asian Americans, and American Indians? (text, pp. 889–892; video segment 4)

19. Who comprised the New Deal Political Coalition? Why did these groups support FDR and the New Deal? What was important about this coalition? (text, p. 893; video segment 4)

20. What role did Eleanor Roosevelt play in the New Deal? (text, pp. 869, 890; video segment 4)

21. Why and how did FDR attempt to "pack" the Supreme Court? What were the results of his effort? (text, p. 894; video segment 4)

22. Why did the economy slump in 1937-1938? How did John Maynard Keynes propose that the government manage the economy? What significant reforms took place in the farm and housing sectors in 1938? (text, pp. 894–896)

23. How did FDR shape the modern presidency? (text, pp. 896–899; video segments 4, 5)

24. In summary, how and why did FDR and the New Deal transform America? (text, all pages; video, all segments)

HISTORICAL EXPERTS INTERVIEWED

Kevin Boyle, Associate Professor, Ohio State University, Columbus, OH
Donald Fixico, Thomas Bowler Distinguished Professor of American Indian History, University of Kansas, Lawrence, KS
Joan Hoff, Research Professor of History, Montana State University, Bozeman, MT
David Kennedy, Professor of History, Stanford University, Stanford, CA
Nelson Lichtenstein, Professor of History, University of California, Santa Barbara, CA

FEATURED FAMILY MEMBERS INTERVIEWED

Edward Archuleta, Santa Fe, NM
Vine Deloria, Jr., Golden, CO
Dianne Swann-Wright, Lake Monticello, VA

PRACTICE TEST

The following items will help you evaluate your understanding of this lesson. Use the Answer Key at the end of the lesson to check your answers or to locate material related to each question.

Multiple Choice: Choose the letter of the best answer.

1. All of the following were priorities of President Roosevelt when he first took office EXCEPT _____.
    A. the economic recovery of business and farming
    B. relief for the unemployed and the destitute
    C. reform of the stock market
    D. civil rights legislation to end the practice of lynching

2. The Federal Deposit Insurance Corporation _____.
    A. was one of Herbert Hoover's most effective responses to bank failures
    B. guaranteed bank customers that the federal government would reimburse them for deposits if their bank failed
    C. closed the nation's banks until they were solvent again
    D. initially covered deposits of $100,000 or more

3. The Civilian Conservation Corps was developed by the Roosevelt administration to _____.
    A. provide work for young women so that they could help support their families
    B. give young men jobs on conservation projects
    C. pay workers in surplus food donated by farmers
    D. conserve natural resources through recycling programs

4. During his first "Hundred Days" in office, President Franklin D. Roosevelt _____.
    A. gave hope to the American people
    B. overthrew the basic capitalist system
    C. installed John Maynard Keynes as Secretary of Treasury
    D. failed to make any meaningful reforms.

5. Although government allotments under the Agricultural Adjustment Act greatly benefited some farmers, the program did not address the needs of _____.
    A. ranchers
    B. cotton plantation owners
    C. tenant farmers and sharecroppers
    D. fruit growers

6. The Works Progress Administration, which operated from 1935 to 1943, _____.
   A. provided low-cost loans to millions of Americans
   B. generated jobs for thirteen million unemployed men and women
   C. set strict limits on the kind of work that qualified for government assistance
   D. was established to put American craftspeople to work

7. After a confrontation at the AFL convention in 1935, _____.
   A. Franklin D. Roosevelt authorized federal troops to shut down the meeting
   B. John L. Lewis proceeded to organize the CIO
   C. Frances Perkins became Secretary of Labor
   D. Henry Ford immediately recognized the United Auto Workers

8. The Social Security Act of 1935 provided _____.
   A. old-age pensions, aid for dependent children, and unemployment insurance
   B. national health insurance, Medicare, and Medicaid
   C. death, disability, and survivor benefits for veterans
   D. workers' compensation, minimum wages, and limits on work hours

9. The New Deal Political Coalition consisted of all of the following EXCEPT _____.
   A. organized labor
   B. business executives
   C. minorities
   D. progressive intellectuals

10. One of the most impressive achievements of the New Deal was _____.
    A. that the United States did not abandon democracy to confront the nation's economic crisis
    B. that it stabilized agriculture in the United States through the end of the century
    C. its strengthening of the military-industrial complex
    D. the privatization of Social Security

Short Answer: Your answer should specifically address the points indicated in one or two paragraphs.

11. To what extent did racial and ethnic minorities benefit from New Deal programs?

12. What was the New Deal Political Coalition? Why was it important?

13. Why do many commentators believe FDR and the New Deal "saved" capitalism in America?

Essay Question: Your response should be several paragraphs long. Your answer should elaborate on the points indicated in a manner that expresses understanding of the material.

14. How and why did FDR and the New Deal fundamentally transform America? In your answer, consider the changes related to business, farmers, laborers, minorities, and politics. What were the limits of the New Deal? What was its legacy?

ANSWER KEY

	Answer	Learning Objectives	Focus Points	References
1.	D	LO 1	FP 3	Text, pp. 868–869
2.	B	LO 1	FP 4	Text, pp. 872–873
3.	B	LO 1	FP 5	Text, pp. 873–875
4.	A	LO 1	FP 8	Text, pp. 868–877; video segment 1
5.	C	LO 4	FP 10	Text, pp. 880–882
6.	B	LO 2	FP 12	Text, pp. 884–886
7.	B	LO 2	FP 14	Text, pp. 886–887; video segment 2
8.	A	LO 2	FP 16	Text, pp. 888–889; video segment 3
9.	B	LO 3	FP 19	Text, p. 893; video segment 4
10.	A	LO 4	FP 24	Text, p. 898

11. .... LO 4 .... FP 18 .... Text, pp. 889–892, video segment 4
    - Consider the situation of African Americans, Hispanic Americans, Asian Americans, and Native Americans.
    - Did African Americans participate in government programs? Did segregation end?
    - How were the lives of Mexican Americans and Asian Americans changed?
    - What was the New Deal for American Indian?

12. .... LO 3 .... FP 19 .... Text, p. 893; video segment 4
    - What interest groups were included?
    - Why did these groups support the New Deal?
    - How did this shift the balance of political power?

13. .... LO 4 .... FP 24 .... Text, pp. 888–899; video segment 5
    - Consider the severity of the economic crisis of the Great Depression
    - What options were being followed in other countries?
    - How did the New Deal programs enable the basic tenets of capitalism to survive?

14. ....LO 4.....................FP 24......................................Text, all pages; video segments 1–5
    - Consider how key financial operations like banking and the stock market were changed.
    - How did New Deal farm programs break new ground?
    - Consider the effects of the Wagner Act, the Social Security Act, and the Fair Labor Standards Act.
    - How were minorities affected by the New Deal and New Dealers?
    - What fundamental shifts took place regarding the presidency and partisan politics?
    - How did the American political tradition and staying within the boundaries of capitalism limit options?
    - How was the relationship of the American people with their government and each other changed?

ENRICHMENT IDEAS

These activities are not required unless your instructor assigns them. They are offered as suggestions to help you learn more about the material presented in this lesson.

1. In a well-reasoned essay, identify the three greatest and the three worst presidents of the United States since 1877. Explain fully, giving a rationale for your selections and drawing conclusions about what determines a president's success or failure.

2. FDR was quoted as saying, "We ought to have two real parties—one liberal and one conservative." Describe and explain the advantages and/or disadvantages of such a party realignment and state your conclusions about the proposal.

3. Social Security has been the bedrock of the American welfare system since 1935. In the early twenty-first century, much attention was given to reforming Social Security. In a thoughtful essay, describe what the Social Security system has meant to Americans. Then explain the main issues involved today and how you would address them.

4. Research the minimum wage in America in the early twenty-first century. In a report on your findings, explain the debates surrounding this issue. What is your position on making the minimum wage a living wage?

SUGGESTED READINGS/RESOURCES

See the "Bibliography" on page 899 of the text if you wish to examine other books and resources related to the material discussed in this lesson.

Lesson 13

Road to War

OVERVIEW

Historians agree that the road to World War II can be found in the carnage of World War I. In the United States, disillusionment coming out of the Great War prompted a retreat from active leadership in world affairs. Although issues like communism, disarmament, relations with Latin America, and renewed aggression could not be ignored, American policymakers made clear in the mid-1930s that the United States intended to stay out of the impending crisis in Europe. When war did break out there in 1939, the United States declared its neutrality. Yet, by 1941, this neutrality was eroding quickly as President Franklin D. Roosevelt and his advisers began turning the United States into the "arsenal of democracy."

The Japanese attack on the United States naval base at Pearl Harbor, Hawaii, was the immediate cause of American entry into World War II. The attack outraged the American people, and they rallied around the flag. Ironically, while fighting for "freedom," fears of Japan and its people helped justify the internment of 112,000 Japanese Americans. The American Civil Liberties Union, one of the few organizations to protest the move, called this action "the greatest single assault on the Constitution in the nation's history."

Meanwhile, the mobilization of the American economic and military forces proceeded. It was apparent from the outset that this war would be more costly than World War I. However, government military spending brought an end to economic depression and opened up economic opportunities for minorities, including women. American resources, human and material, would be a key to the ultimate outcome of the war—a war that transformed America at home as well as in the world arena.

LESSON ASSIGNMENT

Text: Roark, et.al., *The American Promise*
- Chapter 23, "From New Era to Great Depression," pp. 828–829
- Chapter 25, "The United States and the Second World War," pp. 902–929, 942

Video: "Road to War," from the series, *Transforming America*

LEARNING OBJECTIVES

This lesson examines the diplomatic road to World War II, the Japanese attack on Pearl Harbor, and the effects of wartime mobilization on the American people. Upon completion of this lesson, you should be able to:

1. Explain the main features of American foreign policy prior to the attack on Pearl Harbor.

2. Analyze the Japanese attack on Pearl Harbor and its consequences.

3. Analyze the process of wartime mobilization and its effects on the American people.

4. Assess how wartime mobilization transformed America.

LESSON FOCUS POINTS

The following questions are designed to help you get the most benefit from the sources selected for this lesson. For reference purposes, the video is divided into five segments: (1) Introduction, (2) "A Common Purpose," (3) "This Means War," (4) "The Great Arsenal of Democracy," and (5) Summary Analysis: "It Didn't Matter Who You Were."

1. Why was the United States unable to retreat to total isolationism in the 1920s? How did the United States stay involved in world affairs? (text, pp. 828–829)

2. Why did President Franklin D. Roosevelt extend diplomatic recognition to the USSR in 1933? Why did he stay on the sidelines when Germany and Japan became more aggressive in the 1930s? (text, p. 905)

3. Why did the United States undertake a Good Neighbor Policy toward Latin America in the 1930s? What were the main features of this policy? (text, pp. 905–906)

4. Why did the United States pass a series of neutrality laws between 1935–1937? What were the main provisions of this legislation? Why was FDR's "quarantine" speech controversial? (text, pp. 906–907)

5. Why did Adolf Hitler become aggressive in Europe in the late 1930s? How did American and European diplomats respond? Why did World War II begin in September 1939? (text, pp. 908–909; video introduction, segment 2)

6. What did the German "blitzkrieg" mean? What effect did it have on the war? (text, pp. 909–910; video segment 2)

7. How and why did the United States move from neutrality to the arsenal of democracy between 1939-1941? What were the major steps in this process? How did American isolationists respond to this shift? (text, pp. 910–912; video segment 2)

8. What was important about the Atlantic Charter meeting and the charter itself? (text, p. 912; video segments 1, 2)

9. Why did Japan attack the American fleet at Pearl Harbor? Why was the United States caught by surprise? Why was the attack a tactical success and a strategic and operational failure for Japan? (text, pp. 912–913; video segment 3)

10. What were the immediate effects of the Pearl Harbor attack? How did the U.S. initiate home-front security? (text, pp. 914–917; video segment 3)

11. Why and how did the United States intern Japanese Americans? How did this internment affect Japanese Americans? (text, pp. 915–917; video segment 3)

12. How did the United States expand the armed forces? How was discrimination dealt with in the military forces? (text, p. 918; video segment 3)

13. How did the United States organize its economic mobilization efforts? What were the economic results? (text, pp. 918–921, 924–926; video segment 4)

14. How were women's lives affected by the war? How did most families experience and cope with sacrifice? (text, pp. 925–926; video segment 4)

15. What did Latinos and African Americans experience on the home front during World War II? What was important about Executive Order 8802? What is significant about the Double V campaign? (text, pp. 926–927; video segment 4)

16. How did the wartime mobilization affect American politics? What were the provisions of the GI Bill? What was important about the 1944 presidential election? (text, pp. 927–928)

17. In summary, how and why was the United States drawn into World War II? How and why did mobilization for the war transform American society, including its economy? (text, all pages; video segments 1–5)

HISTORICAL EXPERTS INTERVIEWED

Clayborne Carson, Professor of History and Editor of Martin Luther King, Jr. Papers, Stanford University, Stanford, CA
Calvin L. Christman, Professor, Cedar Valley College, Lancaster, TX
Donald Fixico, Thomas Bowler Distinguished Professor of American Indian History, University of Kansas, Lawrence, KS
Susan Hartmann, Professor of History, Ohio State University, Columbus, OH
Akira Iriye, Professor of History, Harvard University, Cambridge, MA
David Kennedy, Professor of History, Stanford University, Stanford, CA
Adrian Lewis, Professor of Military History, University of North Texas, Denton, TX
Guadalupe San Miguel, Jr., Professor of History, University of Houston, Houston, TX
Alice Yang Murray, Associate Professor, University of California, Santa Cruz, CA

FEATURED FAMILY MEMBERS INTERVIEWED

Vine Deloria, Jr., Golden, CO
Eddie Fung, Santa Cruz, CA
Charlene McAden, Blooming Grove, TX
Dianne Swann-Wright, Lake Monticello, VA

PRACTICE TEST

The following items will help you evaluate your understanding of this lesson. Use the Answer Key at the end of the lesson to check your answers or to locate material related to each question.

Multiple Choice: Choose the letter of the best answer.

1. Roosevelt's good-neighbor policy was designed to _____.
   A. replace the country's often belligerent relationship with Latin America with a more cooperative one
   B. funnel billions of dollars into Latin America, a tacit admission that the United States had essentially ruined the economies there
   C. buy property and raw materials from Latin American nations instead of sending in the marines to take those resources
   D. drop restrictions on immigration to the United States from Latin America

2. In the video, "Road to War," Professor Calvin L. Christman makes the point that Adolf Hitler wanted war in the 1930s in order to do all of the following EXCEPT _____.
   A. remake the map of Europe
   B. eradicate Jews
   C. destroy communism
   D. gain control over oil supplies in the Middle East

3. The Lend-Lease Act of 1941 was calculated to _____.
   A. loan France huge sums of money in return for U.S. naval bases in areas controlled by the French
   B. make armaments available to Britain
   C. loan Latin American countries large sums of money in return for U.S. army bases in trouble spots in the Western Hemisphere
   D. make armaments available to Canada

4. The attack on Pearl Harbor on December 7, 1941, was part of the Japanese plan to _____.
   A. knock out American naval bases in the Pacific
   B. demonstrate that the United States could not possibly win a war against an Asian nation
   C. demonstrate to the Germans that Japan had its own objectives in the Pacific
   D. retaliate against the United States for the incarceration of Japanese citizens

5. Internment of Japanese Americans _____.
   A. left deep psychological wounds on those detained
   B. justified the attack on Pearl Harbor
   C. was not authorized by President Roosevelt
   D. was later ruled unconstitutional by the Supreme Court

6. During World War II, members of ethnic minorities in America _____.
   A. were largely uninterested in serving in the armed forces
   B. were barred from jobs in the defense industry
   C. fought in large numbers in the armed forces
   D. were barred from serving in the armed forces

7. By the end of the war, the nation's efforts to mobilize the economy had resulted in _____.
   A. more jobs than there were workers to fill them
   B. manufacturing plants operating at full capacity
   C. a federal budget of more than $100 billion
   D. all of the above

8. In authorizing the Committee on Fair Employment Practices, President Roosevelt _____.
   A. made equal rights for women his top priority
   B. risked offending his southern political allies
   C. had to promise not to seek a fifth term as president
   D. was promising to limit the number of women and minorities in top government positions

9. In the video, "Road to War," a theme common to people remembering World War II was _____.
   A. upward mobility
   B. opposition to the war
   C. spirit of sacrifice
   D. fear of internal subversives

Short Answer: Your answers should specifically address the points indicated in one or two paragraphs.

10. How and why did the United States move closer to war between November 1939 and March 1941?

11. Why did Japan attack Pearl Harbor? Was the attack a victory or miscalculation on the part of Japanese leaders?

12. Why did the United States place Japanese Americans in internment camps during World War II? What were the effects of the camps on Japanese Americans?

13. How were American families affected by World War II?

Essay Questions: Your responses should be several paragraphs long. Your answers should elaborate on the points indicated in a manner that expresses understanding of the material.

14. Explain the major foreign policy decisions of the United States between 1935 and Japan's attack on Pearl Harbor. Why were American efforts to avoid another war unsuccessful?

15. How and why did the mobilization of the United States for participation in World War II transform American society in general and the American economy in particular? In your answer, be sure to consider both short- and long-term effects.

ANSWER KEY

	Answer	Learning Objectives	Focus Points	References
1.	A	LO 1	FP 3	Text, pp. 905–906
2.	D	LO 1	FP 5	Video segment 2
3.	B	LO 1	FP 7	Text, pp. 911–912; video segment 2
4.	A	LO 2	FP 9	Text, pp. 912–913; video segment 3
5.	A	LO 2	FP 11	Text, pp. 915–917; video segment 3
6.	C	LO 3	FP 12	Text, p. 918; video segment 3
7.	D	LO 3	FP 13	Text, pp. 918–921, 924–926; video segment 4
8.	B	LO 3, 4	FP 15	Text, p. 927
9.	C	LO 3	FP 14	Video segment 4

10. ....LO 1.....................FP 7......................................Text, pp. 910–912; video segment 2
- Consider the situation in Europe during this time.
- How was additional help given to Britain (from cash and carry to Lend-Lease)

11. ....LO 2.....................FP 9......................................Text, pp. 912–913; video segment 3
- What was Japan trying to accomplish?
- To what degree was it a tactical success?
- Why was it a strategic and operational failure?

12. ....LO 2, 3..................FP 11......................................Text, pp. 915–917; video segment 3
- What role did fear and prejudice play?
- What rights did they lose?
- What hardships did they endure?

13. ....LO 3, 4..................FP 14......................................Text, pp. 925–926; video segment 4
- What sacrifices did most families make?
- How did families cope?
- What opportunities became available?

14. ....LO 1......................FP 4–9...............................Text, pp. 906–913; video segments 1–3
    - Why did the United States pass neutrality legislation? What provisions were included?
    - How and why did the United States begin to back away from strict neutrality?
    - How did the Atlantic Charter meeting reflect American involvement?
    - Consider U.S. policy toward Japan before Pearl Harbor.
    - What conclusions can you draw about American diplomacy at this time?

15. ....LO 2–4................FP 10–17...................Text, pp. 914–928, 942; video segments 3–5
    - Explain the mobilization process. How was it undertaken?
    - What were the economic results of mobilization?
    - How were families affected? What sacrifices were made?
    - How were minorities, including women, affected?
    - Assess the meaning of the changes brought about.

ENRICHMENT IDEAS

These activities are not required unless your instructor assigns them. They are offered as suggestions to help you learn more about the material presented in this lesson.

1. Interview a family member and/or do research on how World War II affected your family on the home front. Report your findings and include your conclusions about the effects of the war on your family.

2. Research how American involvement in World War II affected the community in which you live. Submit a well-developed essay in which you report on your investigation. (Cite your sources.)

3. Read the "Documenting the American Promise" section of the text concerning "Japanese Internment." (pp. 916–917) Then submit a report in which you thoroughly answer the questions posed in the text.

4. Research the issue of reparations for Japanese Americans interred during World War II. In a well-developed essay, analyze how this issue was addressed and resolved. (Cite your sources.)

SUGGESTED READINGS/RESOURCES

See the "Bibliography" on pages 942–943 of the text if you wish to examine other books and resources related to the material discussed in this lesson.

Lesson 14

World at War

OVERVIEW

While Americans at home produced materials essential for Allied victory in World War II, American military forces engaged the Axis enemies on two fronts. In the Pacific, American forces stopped Japanese advances in mid-1942 and then began the long hard push back to the Japanese mainland. In Europe, American forces joined the Allies in their efforts to squeeze the life out of Italian Fascists and German Nazis. Hard-fought and costly successes in North Africa, Italy, and the Soviet Union, plus the dramatic D-Day invasion, had Germany reeling and caught in a closing pincers movement. As the war wound down in Europe, the public became aware of the extent of the horrible German atrocities against the Jews.

The successful wartime strategy and diplomacy outlined by Franklin D. Roosevelt, British Prime Minister Winston Churchill, and Soviet Premier Joseph Stalin reached their climax at Yalta in February, 1945. Agreements were reached on the fate of Germany, the settlement of boundary and political questions in postwar Eastern Europe, the prosecution of the war against Japan, and the establishment of the United Nations. Germany surrendered in May, 1945, and three months later the United States used atomic bombs to end the war in the Pacific.

Americans would remember World War II as the "good" war. The evil Axis powers had been vanquished. While the cost had been high, America emerged as an economic and military "superpower." Why had this happened? What did it all mean? To what extent had freedom been secured once again?

LESSON ASSIGNMENT

Text: Roark, et. al., *The American Promise*
- Chapter 25, "The United States and the Second World War," pp. 902–904, 921–924, and 928–945

Video: "World at War" from the series *Transforming America*

LEARNING OBJECTIVES

This lesson examines the diplomacy and the military operations of World War II, the holocaust, and the consequences of the war. Upon completing this lesson, you should be able to:

1. Explain the diplomatic decisions and military operations that led to Allied victory in World War II.

2. Analyze American responses to the holocaust.

3. Analyze the use of the atomic bombs and the effects of that decision.

4. Assess the effects of the war on America and the rest of the world.

LESSON FOCUS POINTS

The following questions are designed to help you get the most benefit from the sources selected for this lesson. For reference purposes, the video is divided into five segments: (1) Introduction, (2) "Unconditional Surrender," (3) "The Final Solution," (4) "These Proceedings are Closed," and (5) Summary Analysis: "At the Summit of the World."

1. Who were the Allied Powers in World War II? Who were the Axis Powers? (text, pp. 933, 938)

2. What factors shaped Allied strategy in World War II? Why did the Allies insist on "unconditional surrender" of the Axis? (text, pp. 921–924; video segment 2)

3. What was meant by a "second front" in the European theater of the war? Why was there controversy among the Allies on this point? (text, p. 923; video segment 2)

4. What success did the Allies have in North Africa and Italy in 1942-1943? (text, pp. 923–924; video segment 2)

5. Why was the outcome of the Battle of Stalingrad a critical turning point in World War II? (text, p. 929; video segment 2)

6. What were the effects of the Allied air strikes on Germany in 1942-1944? (text, pp. 929–931; video segment 2)

7. What was the importance of Operation Overlord? What was General Dwight Eisenhower's role in this operation? Why was the D-Day invasion so difficult? (text, pp. 931–934; video segment 2)

8. Examine Map 25.4 on page 933 of the textbook. Answer the questions below the map. (text, p. 933)

9. What was significant about the Battle of the Bulge? (text, pp. 933–935)

10. What arrangements were made at the Yalta Conference? Why were these arrangements significant? (text, pp. 934–935; video segment 2)

11. In the end, why did the Allies defeat Italy and Germany? (text, pp. 932–937; video segment 2)

12. Why and how did Adolf Hitler try to rid Germany of Jews? What was Kristallnacht? Why did the United States and other countries refuse to provide refuge for the Jews prior to World War II? (text, pp. 928–931; video segment 3)

13. Why did Albert Einstein flee Germany in the 1930s? How did this lead to the development of the atomic bomb by the United States? (text, pp. 930–931)

14. Why did it take the Allies so long to respond to the Nazi death camps? What could they do? What were the results of the Holocaust? (text, pp. 928–931; video segment 3)

15. Why was the Battle of Midway a turning point in the Pacific theater of the war? (text, pp. 921–923; video segment 4)

16. How did the American forces proceed to close in on the Japanese mainland from 1943 to mid-1945? Why was the fighting so fierce? What happened at Okinawa? (text, pp. 935–940; video segment 4)

17. Examine Map 25.5 on page 938 of the textbook. Answer the questions below the map. (text, p. 938)

18. How did the United States develop the atomic bomb? Why were the Soviets not included in the process? (text, pp. 931, 940–941)

19. What happened at the Potsdam Conference in July, 1945? (text, pp. 940–941; video segment 4)

20. Why did President Truman authorize the use of atomic bombs on Japan in August, 1945? What role did Paul Tibbets play? What were the results? (text, pp. 902–904, 940–942; video segment 4)

21. In summary, why did the Allies win World War II? What were the costs of the war? How was America transformed at home? How was the world, and the place of the United States in it, transformed? (text, all pages; all video segments)

HISTORICAL EXPERTS INTERVIEWED

Calvin L. Christman, Professor of History, Cedar Valley College, Lancaster, TX
Leonard Dinnerstein, Professor of History, Emeritus, University of Arizona, Tucson, AZ
Akira Iriye, Professor of History, Harvard University, Cambridge, MA
David Kennedy, Professor of History, Stanford University, Stanford, CA
Adrian Lewis, Professor of Military History, University of North Texas, Denton, TX

FEATURED FAMILY MEMBERS INTERVIEWED

Harry Dingenthal, Garland, TX
Eddie Fung, Santa Cruz, CA

PRACTICE TEST

The following items will help you evaluate your understanding of this lesson. Use the Answer Key at the end of the lesson to check your answers or to locate material related to each question.

Multiple Choice: Choose the letter of the best answer.

1. Allied strategists in World War II decided to _____.
   A. defeat the Japanese before challenging the Germans
   B. deter the threat of a German invasion of the Soviet Union
   C. prepare for the possibility that Germany might invade the United States
   D. concentrate their forces against the Germans first

2. The Allies insisted on unconditional surrender of the enemy in World War II because they _____.
   A. thought a mistake was made by not doing so in World War I
   B. wanted to promote democracy in the Soviet Union
   C. needed a good reason to use atomic weapons
   D. believed that Germany would pay war reparations

3. A contentious issue among the Allied leaders during the early years of the war centered around _____.
   A. liberating the Jews from Nazi death camps
   B. establishing a second front against Germany
   C. supporting an anti-communist movement in the Soviet Union
   D. when and where to use atomic weapons

4. The outcome of the Battle of Stalingrad was significant because _____.
   A. Russia could now go on the offensive against the Germans
   B. Germany was relieved from defending its eastern front
   C. Stalin began to lose significant support at home
   D. Hitler had proven his army was superior to that of Napoleon

5. The primary significance of Operation Overlord and D-Day was that it _____.
   A. forced the surrender of Italy
   B. resulted in relatively few Allied casualties
   C. opened a second front against Hitler's forces
   D. illustrated General George Patton's military brilliance

6. One of the keys to Allied victory over Germany was _____.
   A. liberating the Nazi death camps in a timely manner
   B. maintaining effective coordination of their strategy throughout the war
   C. inciting a strong resistance to Hitler inside Germany
   D. developing the atomic bomb

7. All of the following help explain the lack of vigorous action by Franklin Roosevelt's administration regarding the plight of European Jews EXCEPT _____.
   A. widespread anti-Semitic feelings existed in the United States
   B. persecution of the Jews was unknown until the death camps were liberated
   C. many Americans feared massive immigration of Jews
   D. Americans put little effective pressure on the government to take action

8. The Battle of Midway was significant because it _____.
   A. destroyed the Japanese Pacific fleet
   B. allowed the United States to go on the offensive in the Pacific
   C. illustrated the effectiveness of fire bombing the Japanese mainland
   D. brought the Soviet Union into the war against Japan

9. The Japanese defense of Okinawa included the use of _____.
   A. chemical and biological weapons
   B. war prisoners as protection against attack
   C. kamikaze pilots
   D. all of the above

10. The primary reason for using the atomic bombs on Japan was to _____.
    A. demonstrate that the bombs would work
    B. illustrate President Truman's leadership
    C. fulfill an agreement made at Yalta
    D. force Japan to surrender without an Allied invasion

11. One of the most significant results of World War II was that _____.
    A. the United States emerged as a superpower
    B. totalitarianism was banished from the globe
    C. the United States paid the greatest price of all the Allies
    D. equal rights for all were achieved in America

Short Answer: Your answer should specifically address the points indicated in one or two paragraphs.

12. After two years of deliberation, the Allies decided to invade France. Why do you think the slow process of taking action made Stalin angry?

13. What factors kept the United States from helping the victims of Nazi oppression during the war years?

14. Many scientists asked that the atomic bombs be demonstrated publicly before being dropped on Japan. Why do you think President Truman chose to unleash such awesome devastation instead?

Essay Question: Your response should be several paragraphs long. Your answer should elaborate on the points indicated in a manner that expresses understanding of the material.

15. Analyze the importance of American military forces, political and military leaders, and industry in the defeat of the Axis powers in World War II. How did the war transform the world and the place of the United States in international affairs?

ANSWER KEY

	Answer	Learning Objectives	Focus Points	References
1.	D	LO 1	FP 2	Text, p. 921; video segment 2
2.	A	LO 1	FP 2	Text, p. 923; video segment 2
3.	B	LO 1	FP 3	Text, p. 923; video segment 2
4.	A	LO 1	FP 5	Text, p. 929; video segment 2
5.	C	LO 1	FP 7	Text, pp. 931–934; video segment 2
6.	B	LO 1	FP 11	Text, pp. 932–937; video segment 2
7.	B	LO 2	FP 12	Text, pp. 928–931; video segment 3
8.	B	LO 1	FP 15	Text, pp. 921–923; video segment 4
9.	C	LO 1	FP 16	Text, p. 939; video segment 4
10.	D	LO 3	FP 20	Text, pp. 940–942; video segment 4
11.	A	LO 4	FP 21	Text, p. 942; video segment 5

12. ....LO1......................FP 2-3......................................Text, pp. 921–924; video segment 2
    - Consider what role the Soviet Union was playing in the war.
    - Which country was suffering the most casualties?
    - Why did FDR and Churchill decide on North African and Italian invasions first?

13. .... LO2.....................FP 12-14...............................Text, pp. 928–931; video segment 3
    - Consider anti-Semitism within the United States.
    - Why was there lack of political support for changing immigration laws?
    - How did military strategy factor into decisions?

14. .... LO3......................FP 18-20................................ Text, pp. 940–942; video segment 4
    - What were the risks of a demonstration?
    - Why would the bombs save American lives?
    - What effect would the bombs have on the postwar world?

15. .... LO 1-4 ....FP 21 ....Text, pp. 921–924, 928–942; video segments 1-5
    - Consider where American military forces played their most important roles.
    - How did the diplomacy and decisions of FDR and Truman affect the outcome?
    - What military leaders were most significant? Why?
    - How important was American industry?
    - What was the position of the United States at the end of the war?

ENRICHMENT IDEAS

These activities are not required unless your instructor assigns them. They are offered as suggestions to help you learn more about the material presented in this lesson.

1. Interview a veteran of World War II. Then submit a report in which you summarize what you learned from the interviewee regarding the war and how it affected someone who participated.

2. Investigate how your own family was affected by World War II. Then write a brief chapter of your family history based on what you learned.

3. Investigate how the community in which you live was affected by World War II. Report your findings in a well-developed essay.

4. Research how World War II is remembered through monuments and memorials in your area. Then submit a report, including photographs, in which you describe what you found and assess the significance of the monuments and/or memorials.

5. Examine the controversies that have arisen over how World War II is depicted in historical exhibits. One example concerns the *Enola Gay* and the use of atomic bombs against Japan. In a well-developed essay, describe what you discovered about the controversy and what that says about the uses of public history.

SUGGESTED READINGS/RESOURCES

See the "Bibliography" on pages 942–943 of the text if you wish to examine other books and resources related to this lesson.

Unit II: Fiction and Film

Recommended novels and films set in first half of the twentieth century:

The Jungle, by Upton Sinclair. This classic novel about workers in the meatpacking industry led to the passage of the Pure Food and Drug Act and a bill mandating the federal inspection of meat.

The Great Gatsby, by F. Scott Fitzgerald. A portrait of the Jazz Age in all of its decadence and excess, it captured the spirit of the author's generation and earned itself a permanent place in American mythology.

Their Eyes Were Watching God, by Zora Neale Hurston. A luminous and haunting novel, rooted in black folk traditions and steeped in mythic realism, about the journey of a Southern black woman in the 1930s from a free-spirited girl to a woman of independence and substance.

The Grapes of Wrath, by John Steinbeck. This Pulitzer Prize-winning novel brought Depression-era America face to face with itself in a startling, lyrical way. Steinbeck gathered the country's recent shames and devastations in one family of farmers, fleeing the Oklahoma Dust Bowl in hopes of finding a better life in California.

The Winds of War and *War and Remembrance*, by Herman Wouk. A sweeping epic of World War II, Wouk's spellbinding narrative captures the tide of global events, even as it immerses us in the lives of a single American family drawn into the very center of the war's maelstrom.

Inherit The Wind, d. Stanley Kramer. A slightly fictionalized account of the Scopes Monkey Trail, the galvanizing legal drama of the 1920s in which a young Tennessee teacher is put on trial for teaching evolution in the public school.

Modern Times, d. Charlie Chaplin. In this legendary satire of the mechanized world, Chaplin is in glorious form as he executes a series of slapstick routines around machines, including a memorable encounter with an automatic feeding apparatus.

Bonnie And Clyde, d. Arthur Penn. In this poetic ode to the Great Depression, folk heroes Bonnie Parker and Clyde Barrow barrel across the 1930s South, robbing banks and living dangerously. An unforgettable classic that has lost none of its power since its 1967 release.

Bridge on the River Kwai, d. David Lean. Powerful, intelligent, and absorbing, Lean's anti-war epic centers on a Japanese prison camp deep in the jungles of Southeast Asia, where British and American POWs toil on the infamous Burma railway.

Schindler's List, d. Steven Spielberg. This film chronicles Oskar Schindler's spiritual odyssey from war profiteer to humanitarian and hero as he attempts to rescue more than a thousand Jews from Hitler's "Final Solution." Filmed in Poland with an emphasis on absolute authenticity, Spielberg's masterpiece ranks among the greatest films ever made about the Holocaust.

Unit III

Redefining America
1945–1976
"The New Frontiers?"

15. Cold War
16. Pursuit of Happiness
17. All God's Children
18. Times Are A-Changin'
19. The Vietnam Dilemma
20. The Decline of Liberalism

THEME

Looking backward in 1945, those Americans who survived the hardships of the Great Depression and the sacrifices of World War II could reasonably expect that better times lay ahead. They could look forward to pursuing their dreams in a nation positioned to be dominant in world affairs and poised for economic growth. In the post-World War II era, Americans could shape some new frontiers in what some commentators began to refer to as an "American century."

In the international arena, however, fears of the Soviet Union and the spread of communism shattered the security brought about by victories over Germany and Japan. In response, the Truman administration defined a containment policy that guided actions in Europe, the Middle East, Asia, and Latin America for decades afterward. By the end of American involvement in Vietnam in 1975, however, Americans were reassessing the limits of power abroad.

At home, the economy, spurred by government spending and policy, afforded the opportunity for millions of Americans to seek their versions of happiness. In addition, American minorities renewed their efforts to be included in the expanding definitions of freedom and equality.

The apparent triumph of liberal reform embodied in President Lyndon Johnson's Great Society programs was cut short by the war in Vietnam and social disruption at home. By the time the scandal-ridden President Richard Nixon resigned, Americans were losing faith in their government. New frontiers had been broached, but new boundaries were being defined.

Lesson 15

Cold War

OVERVIEW

This lesson provides us with the opportunity to reflect on our recurring themes of American identity, freedom, and equality. Looking back from 1945, we can see that the definition of Americanism changed during the Great Depression and World War II. Looking forward, we can understand how more Americans are now poised to demand a greater degree of freedom and equality.

In 1945, the United States had unmatched military and economic power. The nation seemed to be perfectly positioned to continue its mission of spreading democracy and capitalism to new frontiers throughout the world.

With all of this national power, the American people might have expected to enjoy an era of confidence and security. Instead, doubt and fear soon clouded the horizons of foreign and domestic affairs. The source of this apprehension was the spread of international communism. The globe quickly became divided between the so-called "free world" and the "communist bloc." A different kind of war began, a "cold war." How and why had this happened? What did it mean? How was the Cold War fought both at home and abroad? What were the consequences?

LESSON ASSIGNMENT

Text: Roark, et.al., *The American Promise*
- Chapter 26, "Cold War Politics in the Truman Years," pp. 946–960, 970–981
- Chapter 27, "The Politics and Culture of Abundance," pp. 983–985, 988–995

Video: "Cold War," from the series *Transforming America*

LEARNING OBJECTIVES

This lesson examines the status of American identity, freedom, and equality in 1945 and the causes and consequences of the Cold War in the period 1945-1960. Upon completion of this lesson, you should be able to:

1. Analyze the status of American identity, freedom, and equality in 1945.

2. Explain the origins of the Cold War, the development of the containment policy, and the application of the containment policy in Europe.

3. Explain how the Cold War affected American defense strategy and policy decisions in Asia, the Middle East, and Latin America.

4. Analyze the causes and consequences of the domestic "Red Scare" of the late 1940s and 1950s.

5. Assess the benefits and costs of the Cold War.

LESSON FOCUS POINTS

The following questions are designed to help you get the most benefit from the sources selected for this lesson. For reference purposes, the video is divided into five segments: (1) Introduction/ Unit III Open, (2) "The Iron Curtain," (3) "The Third World," (4) "The Enemy Within," and (5) Summary Analysis: "A Sense of Purpose."

1. How and why did the Great Depression and World War II transform American identity? Why did this changing identity lead to an expectation of greater freedom and equality at home? (video segment 1)

2. Why was America becoming the leader of the "free world?" What did that mean? How and why would assuming leadership of the "free world" also challenge Americans at home? (video segment 1)

3. What explains the emergence of the Cold War? What were the objectives of the United States and the Soviet Union immediately after World War II ended? What were the initial sources of tension? (text, pp. 947–954; video segment 2)

4. How and why did Winston Churchill express his concerns about Soviet actions? How does Map 26.1 in the text illustrate the divisions in postwar Europe? (text, pp. 950–953; video segment 2)

5. What factors shaped President Truman's view of the postwar world? How did Dean Acheson and George Kennan help formulate American policies? (text, pp. 948–951, 954; video segment 2)

6. What was the containment policy? Why was it important? Why did Henry A. Wallace criticize it? (text, pp. 951–954; video segment 2)

7. Why did the United States pursue the Truman Doctrine, the Marshall Plan, and the Berlin Airlift? How did these steps illustrate American commitment to containment? What were the effects of these actions? (text, pp. 954–956; video segment 2)

8. What were the main features of American defense strategy during the Truman administration? Why was NATO important? What was the significance of NSC-68? (text, pp. 956–958, 977; video segment 2)

9. What did the term "third world" mean? Why were there so many national liberation movements in the third world in the postwar era? How did the United States respond to these movements? (text, pp. 958–959; video segment 3)

10. Why did the United States support the creation of Israel in 1948? What were the effects of this decision? (text, pp. 959–960)

11. Why were the Chinese communists able to gain power in 1949? Why was this important? How did the United States respond to this development? (text, pp. 958–959; video segment 3)

12. Why did the Korean War take place? Why was the United States so heavily involved? What were the most important military developments of this war? What were the consequences of war? What conclusions were drawn? (text, pp. 972–978; video segment 3)

13. How and why was President Eisenhower's approach to the Cold War different from that taken by President Truman? What was "brinksmanship?" How did the nuclear arms race affect both foreign and domestic policy? (text, pp. 983–984, 988–989, 994–995; video segment 3)

14. Why and how did the United States intervene in Iran in the 1950s? What were the results of this intervention? (text, p. 991; video segment 3)

15. What was the Suez Crisis? What prompted the "Eisenhower Doctrine?" What did it mean? (text, pp. 991, 994)

16. Why and how did the United States intervene in Guatemala? What were the results of this intervention? Why did the United States end up supporting right-wing dictatorships during this era? (text, pp. 990–991; video segment 3)

17. How did the United States initially deal with the Cuban revolution led by Fidel Castro? What were the results of American and Cuban actions? (text, pp. 990–993; video segment 3)

18. Why did fear of communism within the United States escalate in the late 1940s and early 1950s? How was this fear expressed in the government's loyalty program and the House Un-American Activities Committee? Who were the victims of this Red Scare? Why were Julius and Ethel Rosenberg executed? (text, pp. 970–972; video segment 4)

19. How and why did Senator Joseph McCarthy emerge as such a key figure in this Red Scare? What tactics did he use? Why did his anti-communist crusade eventually collapse? What is the legacy of McCarthyism? (text, 970–972, 985; video segment 4)

20. In summary, why did the Cold War develop after World War II? What were the costs and benefits of the Cold War during the period 1945–1960? How did the Cold War transform America and the world during that era? (text, all pages; video segments 2–5)

HISTORICAL EXPERTS INTERVIEWED

Clayborne Carson, Professor of History and Editor of Martin Luther King, Jr. Papers, Stanford University, Stanford, CA
Eric Foner, Professor of History, Columbia University, New York, NY
David Gutierrez, Professor of History, University of California, San Diego, CA
Fraser Harbutt, Associate Professor, Emory University, Atlanta, GA
Akira Iriye, Professor of History, Harvard University, Cambridge, MA
Alice Kessler-Harris, Professor of History, Columbia University, New York, NY
Walter LaFeber, Professor of History, Cornell University, Ithaca, NY
Patricia Limerick, Faculty Director, Center of the American West, University of Colorado, Boulder, CO
Ellen Schrecker, Professor of History, Yeshiva University, New York, NY
Marilyn Young, Professor of History, New York University, New York, NY

FEATURED FAMILY MEMBERS INTERVIEWED

Edward Archuleta, Santa Fe, NM
Bill Neebe, Wilmette, IL
Judy Yung, Santa Cruz, CA

PRACTICE TEST

The following items will help you evaluate your understanding of this lesson. Use the Answer Key at the end of the lesson to check your answers or to locate material related to this lesson.

Multiple Choice: Choose the letter of the best answer.

1. The Great Depression and World War II affected American identity by _____.
   A. broadening the definition of Americanism to include almost everybody
   B. reinforcing segregation throughout American society
   C. opening America's borders to Asian immigrants
   D. limiting the rights of Americans to travel abroad

2. By 1947, the intense rivalry between the Soviet Union and the United States was being called _____.
   A. the iron curtain
   B. the cold war
   C. Communist hysteria
   D. a postwar rivalry

3. George Kennan thought the application of containment should _____.
   A. be strictly military
   B. involve politics and culture
   C. target China
   D. expire after a few years

4. President Truman responded to the Soviet blockade of West Berlin in 1948 and 1949 by _____.
   A. airlifting more than two million tons of goods to West Berliners
   B. ignoring the blockade
   C. calling Stalin's bluff and sending American soldiers to Germany
   D. asking Congress for a declaration of war

5. In 1949, the United States agreed to join Canada and Western European countries in a collective security alliance called the _____.
   A. Civil Defense Commission
   B. North Atlantic Treaty Organization
   C. Warsaw Pact
   D. Bretton Woods Agreement

6. The United States responded to the fall of the Nationalist government in China by _____.
   A. reluctantly recognizing the People's Republic of China
   B. welcoming the People's Republic of China into the United Nations
   C. sending aid to the Nationalists in Taiwan
   D. all of the above

7. The event that triggered U.S. military action in Korea in 1950 was _____.
   A. the invasion of South Korea by troops from Communist North Korea
   B. Mao Zedong's sending Chinese troops to North Korea
   C. President Truman's firing of General MacArthur
   D. Joseph Stalin's ordering the North Koreans to attack and capture Seoul

8. In 1953, the United States used the CIA to overthrow the Iranian national government in order to _____.
   A. protect American oil interests in the region
   B. spread democracy throughout the Middle East
   C. promote freedom for Iranians
   D. head off a Soviet invasion of the area

9. During the anti-Communist scare of the late 1940s and early 1950s, _____.
   A. many subversives were deported to other countries
   B. federal employees were investigated, people were blacklisted, and homosexuals were harassed
   C. many teachers were jailed for refusing to answer Senate investigators' questions
   D. labor unions were exempt from investigation

10. All of the following were benefits of the Cold War EXCEPT _____.
    A. government spending aided the economy
    B. America's sense of purpose was reinforced
    C. respect for differing opinions increased
    D. Soviet expansion in Europe had been contained

Short Answer: Your answer should specifically address the points indicated in one or two paragraphs.

11. How and why were Americans poised to demand more freedom and equality in the years following World War II?

12. How and why did the United States develop the containment policy in the years after World War II?

13. Why did the CIA assist the overthrow of governments in Iran and Guatemala in the 1950s? What were the results of these actions?

14. What explains the rise and fall of Senator Joseph McCarthy during the Red Scare of the 1940s and 1950s? What is the legacy of McCarthyism?

Essay Question: Your response should be several paragraphs long. Your answer should elaborate on the points indicated in a manner that expresses understanding of the material.

15. Explain the development of the Cold War and the containment policy of the United States. How was the containment policy applied in the 1940s and 1950s? What were the costs and benefits of the Cold War during the period 1945-1960?

ANSWER KEY

	Answer	Learning Objectives	Focus Points	References
1.	A	LO 1	FP 1	Video segment 1
2.	B	LO 2	FP 3	Text, pp. 947–950; video segment 2
3.	B	LO 2	FP 6	Text, pp. 951, 954; video segment 2
4.	A	LO 2	FP 7	Text, pp. 955–956; video segment 2
5.	B	LO 2	FP 8	Text, p. 957
6.	C	LO 3	FP 11	Text, pp. 958–959
7.	A	LO 3	FP 12	Text, pp. 972–973; video segment 3
8.	A	LO 3	FP 14	Text, p. 991; video segment 3
9.	B	LO 4	FP 18	Text, pp. 970–972; video segment 4
10.	C	LO 5	FP 20	Text, pp. 977–978; video segment 5

11. .... LO 1 .... FP 1, 2 .... Video segment 1
    - How did the labor movement raise expectations in the 1930s?
    - Why would participation in the war lead to activism at home?
    - How was freedom and equality being denied within the United States?

12. .... LO 2 .... FP 5, 6 .... Text, pp. 948–954; video segment 2
    - Why did Soviet actions in eastern Europe cause alarm?
    - How did George Kennan propose that Russia expansion be contained?
    - How did the United States implement containment? How did that accomplish American objectives?

13. .... LO 3 .... FP 14, 16 .... Text, pp. 990–991; video segment 3
    - What was the primary interest of the United States in Iran?
    - Why was Arbenz considered a threat in Guatemala?
    - Why did America help install dictatorial regimes? What happened?

14. .... LO 4 .... FP 18, 19 .... Text, pp. 970–972, 985; video segment 4
    - Where did McCarthy come from? What were his motives?
    - What factors gave him ammunition?
    - How was he exposed? How did he affect political discourse?

15. .... LO 2–5 .... FP 20 .... Text, all pages; video segments 2–5
    - What were the origins of the Cold War?
    - What premise is behind containment?
    - How were specific U.S. actions in Europe, the Middle East, and Asia guided by containment?
    - Assess what had been accomplished. At what price?

ENRICHMENT IDEAS

These activities are not required unless your instructor assigns them. They are offered as suggestions to help you learn more about the material presented in this lesson.

1. Read and analyze the "Documenting the American Promise" segment on "The Emerging Cold War" on pages 952–953 of *The American Promise* textbook. Submit a report on that segment in which you thoroughly answer the questions posed in the text.

2. Interview a veteran of the Korean War. Find out how the war affected the life of the veteran. After the interview, write a well-developed report in which you describe your findings and assess the significance of the Korean War on individual lives and on the nation.

3. Investigate the Korean War Memorial in Washington, DC. Then submit a report in which you describe how and why this memorial was established and explain how it memorializes that war.

4. Investigate the case of the "Hollywood Ten." In a well-developed essay, explain who these people were and what happened to them in the late 1940s and 1950s? What does this episode teach us?

SUGGESTED READINGS/RESOURCES

See the "Bibliography" on pages 978–979 and 1016–1017 of the text if you wish to examine other books and resources related to the material discussed in this lesson.

Lesson 16

Pursuit of Happiness

OVERVIEW

While the Cold War dominated American foreign policy in the post-World War II era (1945-1960), the American people were pursuing their versions of happiness at home. For many, that meant a secure job, a new suburban home, a new car, a television, and, by the end of the 1950s, enjoying a hamburger at McDonald's. For others, especially those on the edges of society, this was a time to seek a greater degree of inclusion in the promise of America, or perhaps to express their individuality in the midst of conformity.

Wartime savings, government spending, business expansion, and union wages all contributed to unprecedented economic growth during this era. The nature of work was changing. By 1956, more workers labored in the service sector of the economy than in the manufacturing sector. The irony of American agriculture continued, as thousands of farmers produced themselves out of business; they and/or their children fled to the city for economic and social opportunities.

Cities grew outward, as suburbs sprawled to house the growing population. There, family roles seemed to be clearly defined. Ironically, the popular ideal of married women as homemakers spread at the same time that more of them entered the work force. Television shaped perceptions of life and enticed consumers with new forms of advertising. Automobiles traveling on interstate highways and freeways could take folks almost anywhere in the United States. The American people were on the move, especially to the West and Southwest.

On the fringes of this social landscape, cultural rebels reminded the majority that many were uneasy with the norms of the era. Writers, artists, and musicians sought new forms of expression. Minorities, particularly African Americans, challenged the status quo of segregation and demanded a greater degree of freedom and equality.

Understanding domestic life in America during the period of 1945-1960 enables us to put that era in perspective. It was a significant time of transition after the trying times of depression and war, and what happened then would help shape America for the rest of the century.

LESSON ASSIGNMENT

Text: Roark, et. al., *The American Promise*
- Chapter 26, "Cold War in the Truman Years," pp. 960–970, 975–979
- Chapter 27, "The Politics and Culture of Abundance," pp. 982–988, 996–1019

Video: "Pursuit of Happiness," from the series *Transforming America*

LEARNING OBJECTIVES

This lesson examines domestic life in America in the late 1940s and 1950s. Upon completion of this lesson, you should be able to:

1. Explain the reasons for economic growth, the changing nature of work, and the limitations of prosperity during this era.

2. Assess the major political developments of the period.

3. Analyze the major social trends of the era.

4. Analyze the status of minorities, including their success in challenging segregation.

5. Assess the importance of this era in the transformation of America.

LESSON FOCUS POINTS

The following questions are designed to help you get the most benefit from the sources selected for this lesson. For reference purposes, the video is divided into five segments: (1) Introduction, (2) "Living Large," (3) "The Feminine Mystique," (4) "If We Protest Courageously...," and (5) Summary Analysis: "Happy Days."

1. What were the major challenges existing in the American economy as it converted from wartime to peacetime? How were these challenges addressed? (text, pp. 960–964; video segment 2)

2. Why were there so many labor strikes in 1946? What gains did organized labor make? What effect did higher wages have on the economy? Why was the Taft-Hartley Act passed? How did it affect labor? (text, pp. 960–961, 964, 968, 997–998; video segment 2)

3. How did wartime saving and government spending stimulate the economy? How did the GI Bill affect veterans and the economy? What were the dangers of the military-industrial complex? (text, pp. 960–961, 964, 966–967, 985–986, 995; video segment 2)

4. Why did African Americans, Mexican Americans, Asians, and poor whites not share equally in the prosperity of the era? How did African Americans and Mexican Americans protest their condition? What gains did they make? What was important about the 1952 Immigration Act? (text, pp. 964–965, 968, 970, 997, 1000–1003; video segment 2)

5. What expectations faced women in the postwar era? What was their place in the work force? What was the "feminine mystique?" (text, pp. 960–963, 997–998, 1004; video segment 3)

6. Why did suburbs like Levittown develop? What characterized suburban life? How were cities faring at this time? (text, pp. 998–999; video segment 3)

7. Why did President Truman face political difficulties in the 1948 presidential election? Why did he win? (text, pp. 968–970)

8. Why was Dwight Eisenhower elected president in 1952? What did "modern Republicanism" mean? Why did Eisenhower win a second term? (text, pp. 975–976, 984–986, 988)

9. How and why did the government implement an American Indian program of compensation, termination, and relocation by the 1950s? How did this affect American Indians? (text, pp. 986–988)

10. How did technology transform agriculture and industry in the 1950s? (text, pp. 996–998)

11. What explains the growth of the Sun Belt in this era? How important is air conditioning in this development? (text, pp. 998–1001; video segment 2)

12. To what extent was higher education democratized? What effects did this have on society? (text, p. 1002; video segment 3)

13. What characterized the consumer culture of the 1950s? How did television transform culture and politics? How was a renewed interest in religion expressed? (text, pp. 1003–1006; video segments 1–3)

14. How was cultural dissent expressed in literature, music, and art at this time? (text, pp. 1006–1009)

15. How and why did the African American challenge to discrimination pick up momentum in the late 1940s and 1950s? How did developments in music and sports change attitudes? What role was the federal government playing? (text, pp. 964–965; 1009–1011, 1014–1015; video segment 4)

16. What was the Supreme Court's decision in *Brown v. Board of Education* in 1954? How did the Court arrive at this decision? Why is it so important? (text, pp. 1010–1013; video segment 4)

17. Why was the process of school integration so slow? How did President Eisenhower deal with integration and civil rights issues? Why did he take these positions? What was important about the integration of Central High School in Little Rock, Arkansas? (text, p. 1010–1013)

18. How and why did the Montgomery, Alabama, bus boycott come about in 1955? What were the results of this protest? What is its significance? (text, pp. 1011, 1014–1015; video segment 4)

19. In summary, what explains the major economic, social, cultural, and political developments of the post-World War II era? What is the long-term significance of this era in transforming America? (text, all pages; video segments 1–5)

HISTORICAL EXPERTS INTERVIEWED

Michael Bernstein, Professor of History, University of California, San Diego, CA
Julian Bond, Chairman, NAACP Board of Directors, Washington, DC
Kevin Boyle, Associate Professor, Ohio State University, Columbus, OH
Clayborne Carson, Professor of History and Editor of Martin Luther King, Jr. Papers, Stanford University, Stanford, CA
Dorothy Sue Cobble, Professor of History and Labor Studies, Rutgers University, New Brunswick, NJ
Susan Hartmann, Professor of History, Ohio State University, Columbus, OH
Steven Lawson, Professor of History, Rutgers University, Princeton, NJ
Valinda Littlefield, Assistant Professor, University of South Carolina, Columbia, SC
Michael McGerr, Professor of History, Indiana University, Bloomington, IN
Susan Strasser, Professor of History, University of Delaware, Newark, DE

FEATURED FAMILY MEMBERS INTERVIEWED

Charlene McAden, Blooming Grove, TX
Dianne Swann-Wright, Lake Monticello, VA

PRACTICE TEST

The following items will help you evaluate your understanding of this lesson. Use the Answer Key at the end of the lesson to check your answers or to locate material related to each question.

Multiple Choice: Choose the letter of the best answer.

1. Among the most serious domestic problems facing the United States after World War II were _____.
    A. unemployment and child care
    B. stagflation and unemployment
    C. inflation and labor relations
    D. health care and retirement funding

2. The passage of the Taft–Hartley Act over Truman's veto in 1947 _____.
    A. was a blow to labor
    B. removed all government control over labor unions
    C. was a major victory for labor
    D. was opposed by the Republican Party

3. The founding of the American GI Forum in 1948 and subsequent efforts by Mexican Americans to challenge their segregation in public schools demonstrated the _____.
   A. growing mobilization of Mexican Americans in the Southwest
   B. high level of cooperation between Mexican Americans and blacks following World War II
   C. sharp differences between Mexican Americans and blacks in terms of the racism they confronted after World War II
   D. the growing mobilization of Mexican Americans in the Northeast and South

4. Immediately after World War II, women were expected to _____.
   A. pursue a college education
   B. leave jobs in the manufacturing sector
   C. stay in the military
   D. enter the professions

5. As the first Republican to serve as president after the New Deal, Dwight D. Eisenhower can be credited with _____.
   A. reducing the size and functions of the federal government
   B. protecting corporate interests in every instance
   C. leaving the size and functions of the federal government intact
   D. dismantling social welfare

6. Between 1940 and 1960, the output of farms in the United States increased, and the number of farmworkers _____.
   A. increased proportionately
   B. decreased by nearly one-third
   C. remained essentially the same
   D. fell by one half

7. Many Americans moved to the Sun Belt in the 1950s because _____.
   A. new modes of transportation had made the area more accessible
   B. northern cities had no jobs for displaced farmers
   C. the advent of air-conditioning made it possible to live and work in the region more comfortably
   D. farmwork there paid relatively well

8. In the book, *The Feminine Mystique*, author Betty Friedan put forward the idea that _____.
   A. women should have more choices
   B. the domestic goddess was the perfect role for women
   C. state legislatures were denying women the right to vote
   D. suburban life was more satisfying for women than it appeared

9. The most important changes in civil rights in the 1950s were instigated by _____.
   A. the Supreme Court
   B. white liberals
   C. ordinary African Americans
   D. Congress

10. Developments of the 1950s set the stage for _____.
    A. black and women's protest movements in the 1960s and 1970s
    B. less presence of the federal government in American life
    C. resurgence of the manufacturing sector of the economy
    D. diminishing power of large corporations in society

Short Answer: Your answer should specifically address the points indicated in one or two paragraphs.

11. How and why did organized labor make gains and suffer some losses in the years after World War II? Why were their gains important for the economy?

12. How and why did women's lives reflect popular ideals and economic realities in the 1950s?

13. How and why did television shape the consumer culture of the 1950s?

14. Why was the Montgomery bus boycott successful?

Essay Question: Your response should be several paragraphs long and elaborate on the points indicated in a manner that expresses understanding of the material.

15. Explain the major economic and social developments occurring in America in the period 1946-1960. What is the longer term significance of this era in transforming America?

ANSWER KEY

	Answer	Learning Objectives	Focus Points	References
1.	C	LO 1	FP 1	Text, pp. 960–964; video segment 2
2.	A	LO 1	FP 2	Text, p. 968
3.	A	LO 4	FP 4	Text, p. 968
4.	B	LO 3	FP 5	Text, pp. 960–963; video segment 3
5.	C	LO 2	FP 8	Text, pp. 984–986, 988
6.	B	LO 1	FP 10	Text, pp. 996–998
7.	C	LO 3	FP 11	Text, pp. 998–1001
8.	A	LO 3	FP 5	Text, p. 1004; video segment 3
9.	C	LO 4	FP 15	Text, pp. 1010–1011, 1014–1015; video segment 4
10.	A	LO 5	FP 19	Text, pp. 1015–1016; video segments 4, 5

11. .... L0 1 .... FP 2 .... Text, pp. 960–961, 964, 968, 997–998; video segments 2, 5
    - Consider the role of strikes. How were they settled? What was public reaction?
    - How did the Taft-Hartley Act illustrate a reaction against unions?
    - How did higher union wages help the economy?

12. ....LO 3......................FP 5.........Text, pp. 960–963, 997–998, 1004; video segments 3, 5
    - Why was the ideal of the domestic goddess popular?
    - Why did more married women enter the work force?
    - What types of jobs were typically open to women?

13. ....LO 3......................FP 13...........................Text, pp. 1003–1006; video segments 1–3
    - How widespread was television viewing by the late 1950s?
    - Who paid for television broadcasting?
    - What types of items did television ads promote?

14. ....LO 4......................FP 18......................... Text, pp. 1011, 1014–1015; video segment 4
    - Consider the local support systems in place.
    - What roles did leaders and ordinary citizens play?

15. ....LO 1–5................FP 19.. Text, all; video segments 1–5
    - Consider the economic growth of the time.
    - How did government spending stimulate the economy?
    - Why were people moving to the Sun Belt?
    - How was the car culture expanding?
    - Why did suburbs expand? What effects did this have?
    - How were women and other minorities faring?
    - How did this era provide a transition time in the mid-twentieth century?

ENRICHMENT IDEAS

These activities are not required unless your instructor assigns them. They are offered as suggestions to help you learn more about the material presented in this lesson.

1. If any of your parents or grandparents grew up in the 1950s, interview them to gain insight on your family history as well as the era. Report what you learned in a well-developed essay.

2. Read and analyze the "Documenting the America Promise" feature on "The Brown Decision" in the text (pp. 1012–1013). Answer the questions posed in the text in a thorough essay.

3. Read and analyze Map 27.2 on page 1000 of the text. Answer the questions posed in the text and complete the map activity available at the publisher's web site.

SUGGESTED READINGS/RESOURCES

See the "Bibliography" on pages 978–979 and 1016–1017 of the text if you wish to examine other books and resources related to the material discussed in this lesson.

Lesson 17

All God's Children

OVERVIEW

The pursuit of freedom in America reached a turning point in 1960. Presidential candidate John F. Kennedy spoke of a "New Frontier . . . of unfulfilled hopes and threats." He mentioned the challenges of "unsolved problems of peace and war, unconquered pockets of ignorance and prejudice, unanswered questions of poverty and surplus." Once elected, JFK urged his fellow Americans to help their country fulfill its promise.

African Americans had already begun to broaden their horizons in their pursuit of freedom and equality. Sit-ins were followed by "freedom rides," demonstrations, and marches. Resistance was strong and often violent, but the freedom movement would not be turned around. "Jim Crow" was on the run, and the passage of the Civil Rights Act of 1964 and the Voting Rights Act of 1965 marked a Second Reconstruction of equal rights in America.

Meanwhile, JFK's successor, President Lyndon Johnson, was trying to lead the nation toward a "Great Society." Building upon the foundation established by progressives and New Dealers, LBJ and his liberal supporters launched a "war on poverty" and initiated numerous other social reforms. America's welfare system expanded, but impediments to achieving America's promise remained.

After 1965, the African American freedom movement splintered along generational and philosophical lines. Demands for "black power" and greater economic equality met greater resistance. Riots, sparked by frustrations and lack of tangible progress in social and living conditions, broke out in many cities. The assassinations of Martin Luther King, Jr. and Robert F. Kennedy in 1968 shattered hopes and dreams. The majority of Americans longed for stability, and Richard Nixon's victory in the 1968 presidential election was based in part on his pledge to restore law and order.

Truly, as Professor Bruce Schulman observes in the video for this lesson, "the Civil Rights era tells us something about the triumphs and the limitations of America's faith in the principle of equality." How and why had all of this happened? How was America transformed? What did it all mean?

LESSON ASSIGNMENT

Text: Roark, et. al., *The American Promise*
- Chapter 28, "Reform, Rebellion, and Reaction," pp. 1020–1039, 1057–1061

Video: "All God's Children" from the series *Transforming America*

LEARNING OBJECTIVES

This lesson examines the African American freedom movement and the expansion of social welfare programs during the 1960s. Upon completion of this lesson, you should be able to:

1. Analyze the leadership and tactics of the civil rights movement in the early 1960s.

2. Assess the roles of Presidents John F. Kennedy and Lyndon B. Johnson, Congress, and the Supreme Court in the expansion of civil rights during the 1960s.

3. Analyze the major civil rights and social welfare legislation of the era.

4. Examine why the African American freedom movement splintered and lost momentum after 1965.

5. Assess how the civil rights movement and the Great Society programs of the 1960s transformed America.

LESSON FOCUS POINTS

The following questions are designed to help you get the most benefit from the sources selected for this lesson. For reference purposes, the video is divided into five segments: (1) Introduction, (2) "We Shall Overcome," (3) "The Great Society," (4) "Black Power," and (5) Summary Analysis: "The Right Path."

1. Why did John F. Kennedy win the 1960 presidential election? How and why did President Kennedy and his "New Frontier" inspire Americans? How do historians judge the substance of Kennedy's domestic record? (text, pp. 1023–1025)

2. What was the status of the African American freedom movement in 1960? How and why did the sit-ins and freedom rides give the movement new momentum? (text, pp. 1031–1034, video segment 2)

3. Why was white resistance so strong in the South? How does Fannie Lou Hamer's story illustrate this resistance as well as her courage and determination? How did Southern Democrats in Congress influence the response of the Kennedy administration to civil rights issues? (text, pp. 1021–1023, 1032–1035; video segment 2)

4. Why were the demonstrations during April 1963 in Birmingham, Alabama, effective and important? What was the significance of Martin Luther King's "Letter from the Birmingham Jail?" How did the Kennedy administration respond to the Birmingham situation? (text, p. 1034; video segment 2)

5. What was important about the March on Washington in August 1963? Why is King's "I Have a Dream" speech significant? (text, p. 1034; video segment 1)

6. How did John F. Kennedy's assassination affect the country and the civil rights movement? (text, pp. 1025–1026; video segment 3)

7. What strengths did Lyndon Johnson bring to the presidency? Why did he emerge as a champion of civil rights and social reform? (text, pp. 1025–1028; video segment 3)

8. Why were the Civil Rights Act of 1964 and the Voting Rights Act of 1965 passed? What is important about this legislation? What other steps were taken to ban discrimination during the Johnson administration? (text, pp. 1034–1036; video segment 3)

9. What was President Johnson's vision of a "Great Society?" What were the major features of the Great Society legislation and programs? (text, pp. 1026–1031; video segment 3)

10. Why and how was a "war on poverty" implemented during the Johnson administration? What was important about it? What success did it have? What limited its success? (text, pp. 1026–1031; video segment 3)

11. How did the Supreme Court support equal rights during this era? What were the results of the court's decisions? (text, pp. 1029, 1031)

12. Why did urban riots break out across America in the mid-1960s? What were the results of this turmoil? (text, pp. 1037–1038; video segment 4)

13. What explains the emergence of "black power" advocates in the mid-1960s? What did "black power" mean? What is its legacy? (text, pp. 1037–1039; video segment 4)

14. Why was Malcolm X an intriguing figure in the 1960s? Why was he important? (text, pp. 1038–1039; video segment 4)

15. Why and how did Stokely Carmichael and the Black Panthers represent a more militant and radical approach to issues of freedom and equality? What were the effects of their efforts? (text, pp. 1038–1039; video segment 4)

16. How did the assassinations of Martin Luther King, Jr. and Robert F. Kennedy affect the civil rights movement? (text, p. 1039; video segment 4)

17. In summary, how and why did the civil rights movement and the legislation enacted in the 1960s transform America? What does this era teach us about change in America? (text, all pages; video segments 1–5)

HISTORICAL EXPERTS INTERVIEWED

Julian Bond, Chairman, Board of Directors, NAACP, Washington, DC
Clayborne Carson, Professor of History and Editor of Martin Luther King, Jr. Papers, Stanford University, Stanford, CA
William Chafe, Professor of History, Duke University, Chapel Hill, NC
Steven Lawson, Professor of History, Rutgers University, New Brunswick, NJ
Valinda Littlefield, Assistant Professor of History, University of South Carolina, Columbia, SC
Bruce Schulman, Professor of History, Boston University, Boston, MA

FEATURED FAMILY MEMBERS INTERVIEWED

Dianne Swann-Wright, Lake Monticello, VA
Judy Yung, Santa Cruz, CA

PRACTICE TEST

The following items will help you evaluate your understanding of this lesson. Use the Answer Key at the end of the lesson to check your answers or to locate material related to each question.

Multiple Choice: Choose the letter of the best answer.

1. President Kennedy believed that to eradicate poverty and solve most social problems, the United States needed to _____.
   A. grow the economy
   B. control runaway inflation
   C. have a strong military presence
   D. redistribute wealth through its tax policy

2. In 1961, the Congress of Racial Equality organized Freedom Rides to _____.
   A. transport African American voters to the polls
   B. commemorate the emancipation of slaves in the United States
   C. provide free transportation to poor people of all races in the South
   D. integrate interstate transportation in the South

3. The March on Washington in August 1963 was important because it _____.
   A. illustrated how radicals could take over peaceful protest
   B. gave the civil rights movement great respectability
   C. threatened national security in the nation's capital
   D. disrupted major transportation networks in the East

4. President Lyndon Baines Johnson came to the White House _____.
   A. with little experience in the political arena
   B. with enormous skill in persuading and threatening legislators
   C. without the political power to get the Kennedy legislation passed
   D. committed above all to getting the nation out of the Vietnam conflict

5. The most important factor in the passage of the Civil Rights Act of 1964 was _____.
   A. the Freedom Ride movement
   B. the Mississippi Freedom Summer Project
   C. growing public support for civil rights
   D. the pressure put on Congress by black organizations

6. The Medicare program provided _____.
   A. universal hospital insurance for the elderly
   B. health insurance coverage for all people on welfare
   C. hospital insurance only for those in need
   D. none of the above

7. More people in the black civil rights movement became radicalized when _____.
   A. the realities of economic disparity became more apparent
   B. minority politicians started third parties
   C. Democratic officials refused to back the war on poverty
   D. the Supreme Court became dominated by conservatives

8. By 1966, the principles espoused by Malcolm X had given rise to the _____.
   A. black is beautiful movement
   B. vote black movement
   C. assimilate today movement
   D. black power movement

9. Martin Luther King, Jr. was assassinated on April 4, 1968, while _____.
   A. leading a march in Atlanta
   B. demonstrating on Chicago's south side
   C. supporting a municipal garbage workers' strike in Memphis
   D. giving a speech in Tallahassee

10. The civil rights movement of the 1960s can be considered the most important movement in the twentieth century because it _____.
    A. addressed questions of power, inequality, and mistreatment
    B. eliminated racism in modern America
    C. assured that Democrats would dominate national politics
    D. divided the country along racial and class lines

Short Answer: Your answer should specifically address the points indicated in one or two paragraphs.

11. Why were the civil rights demonstrations in Birmingham, Alabama, in April 1963 effective and important?

12. How successful was the "war on poverty?" Why is poverty such a difficult issue in America?

13. What does the African American civil rights movement of the 1960s teach us about change in America?

Essay Question: Your response should be several paragraphs long and elaborate of the points indicated in a manner that expresses understanding of the material.

14. How and why did the African American civil rights/freedom movement and the social legislation enacted in the 1960s transform America? What does that era teach us about change in America?

ANSWER KEY

	Answer	Learning Objectives	Focus Points	References
1.	A	LO 2	FP 1	Text, pp. 1023–1025
2.	D	LO 1	FP 2	Text, pp. 1031–1034; video segment
3.	B	LO 1	FP 5	Text, p. 1034; video segment 1
4.	B	LO 2	FP 7	Text, pp. 1025–1028; video segment 3
5.	C	LO 3	FP 8	Text, pp. 1034–1036; video segment 3
6.	A	LO 3	FP 9	Text, pp. 1026–1031; video segment 3
7.	A	LO 4	FP 13	Text, pp. 1037–1039; video segment 4
8.	D	LO 4	FP 13, 14	Text, pp. 1037–1039; video segment 4
9.	C	LO 4	FP 16	Text, p. 1039; video segment 4
10.	A	LO 5	FP 17	Video segment 5

11. ....LO 1.................FP 4... Text, p. 1034; video segment 2
    - Consider the significance of the location and the tactics used.
    - What effect did media coverage have?
    - What did the demonstrations force the Kennedy administration to do?

12. ....LO 3, 5.................FP 10.................................. Text, pp. 1026–1031; video segment 3
    - What happened to poverty rates as a result of the war on poverty?
    - Who benefited most? Who benefited least?
    - What would have to be done to reduce poverty further?

13. ....LO 5....................FP 17.......................................Text, all pages; video segments 1–5
    - When does change happen in America? What elements are needed?
    - Consider the roles of leaders, radicals, and ordinary people.
    - What factors limit change?

14. ....LO 5....................FP 17.......................................Text, all pages, video segments 1–5
    - Consider the status of civil rights and freedom in America in 1960.
    - What were the effects of the sit-ins, freedom rides, and demonstrations?
    - Why was significant civil rights legislation enacted?
    - How did the Civil Rights Act of 1964 and the Voting Rights Act of 1965 change America?
    - What were the most significant changes brought about by Great Society legislation?
    - How were attitudes toward race and equal opportunity changed?
    - How does change happen? What limits change?

ENRICHMENT IDEAS

These activities are not required unless your instructor assigns them. They are offered as suggestions to help you learn more about the material presented in this lesson.

1. Interview someone who was active in the African American civil rights movement of the 1960s. Using the interview as a primary source and reflecting upon what you have learned in this lesson, submit a well-developed essay in which you analyze how the civil rights movement brought about change in America.

2. Research the effects of the Voting Rights Act of 1965 and its subsequent extensions in your area. Then submit a thoughtful essay in which you describe your findings and explain how the changes have affected your community.

SUGGESTED READINGS/RESOURCES

See the "Bibliography" on pages 1058–1059 of the text if you wish to examine other books and resources related to the material discussed in this lesson.

Lesson 18

Times Are A-Changin'

OVERVIEW

Our text provides an excellent introduction to the content of this lesson:

> The civil rights movement's undeniable moral claims helped make protest respectable, while its impact on public opinion and government policy encouraged other groups with grievances. Native Americans, Latinos, college students, women, gay men and lesbians, environmentalists, and others drew on the black freedom struggle for inspiration and models of activism. These groups engaged in direct-action protests, expressed their own cultural nationalism, and challenged dominant institutions and values. (*The American Promise*, 4th ed., p. 1039)

Indeed, as a result of this multitude of movements, the times were changing and the definition of freedom was expanding. More college students became more politically active, demanding free speech, and challenging the authority and values of their elders (including those running the Vietnam War). Underscoring what appeared to be a widening generation gap was an emerging counterculture that often shocked the establishment. American Indians engaged in occasional militant and well-publicized protest demonstrations, sought redress in court for treaty violations, and demanded a greater degree of self-determination. The diversified Latino movement was active on many fronts, including the inspiring efforts of Cesar Chavez and Dolores Huerta to organize migrant farm workers. Lastly, and arguably the most significant of all, a new wave of feminism brought about enduring changes in women's roles and rights.

The changes initiated in the 1960s and early 1970s continue to affect almost everyone living in contemporary America. Why and how did this happen? What did it all mean? How was America transformed during this era of activism?

LESSON ASSIGNMENT

Text: Roark, et. al., *The American Promise*
- Chapter 28: "Reform, Rebellion, and Reaction," pp. 1039–1061

Video: "Times Are A-Changin'" from the series *Transforming America*

LEARNING OBJECTIVES

This lesson examines the changes brought about by the student, American Indian, Latino, and women's movements of the 1960s and early 1970s. Upon completion of this lesson, you should be able to:

1. Explain the emergence and the effects of the student movement and the countercultural trends of the era.

2. Assess the causes and consequences of the American Indian movement.

3. Analyze the emergence and success of Latino reform efforts.

4. Analyze the causes and consequences of the feminist movement.

5. Assess how the changes initiated during this era transformed America.

LESSON FOCUS POINTS

The following questions are designed to help you get the most benefit from the sources selected for this lesson. For reference purposes, the video is divided into five segments: (1) Introduction, (2) "Turning Up the Volume," (3) "A Politicized People," (4) "The Second Wave," and (5) Summary Analysis: "A New Platform."

1. Why and how did college students become activists in the 1960s? How did the Students for a Democratic Society (SDS) reflect this activism? What was important about the Port Huron Statement? (text, pp. 1042–1046; video segment 2)

2. Why and how did the "New Left" of the SDS challenge the prevailing liberalism of the era? (text, pp. 1042–1046; video segment 2)

3. What prompted the "free speech" movement? What issues were at stake? What effects did it have? (text, pp. 1043–1045; video segment 2)

4. What was the "counterculture?" How was it expressed? (text, pp. 1043–1046; video segment 2)

5. How and why did the Vietnam War turn the student movement into a mass movement? (video segment 2)

6. Why and how did American Indian activism take on new goals and militancy in the 1960s? How did the National Indian Youth Council (NIYC) and the American Indian Movement (AIM) reflect this growing discontent? What actions did they initiate? (text, pp. 1039–1041; video segment 3)

7. Why did American Indians seize Alcatraz Island in 1969? What brought about the occupation of Wounded Knee in 1973? What were the results of these and other Indian protests of this era? (text, pp. 1040–1041; video segment 3)

8. Who is Vine Deloria? Why was his book, *Custer Died for Your Sins*, important? How does Philip Deloria represent the complexities of cultural identity? (video segment 3)

9. Why and how did Latinos mobilize for social and political change in the 1960s and 1970s? How were their issues and protests similar to those of African Americans and American Indians? Why was the term Chicano particularly meaningful? (text, pp. 1041–1042; video segment 3)

10. Why did Cesar Chavez and Dolores Huerta organize the United Farm Workers? What obstacles did they face? How did they gain support? What success did they have? (text, pp. 1041–1042; video segment 3)

11. What were the consequences of the Latino struggles for justice in the 1960s and 1970s? (text, pp. 1041–1042; video segment 3)

12. Why and how did a new wave of feminism emerge during the 1960s? What issues were at the forefront of the women's movement? (text, pp. 1049–1050; video segment 4)

13. What was important about the President's Commission on the Status of Women? What was significant about the Equal Pay Act of 1963? (text, pp. 1050–1051)

14. Why was Title VII included in the Civil Rights Act of 1964? What was important about it? (text, p. 1051; video segment 4)

15. Why was the National Organization for Women (NOW) formed? What were its goals? How did it try to bring about change? (text, p. 1051; video segment 4)

16. What was the decision of the Supreme Court in *Roe v. Wade*? Why were the effects of this decision important? (text, p. 1053; video segment 4)

17. Initially, what distinguished "radical" feminists from mainstream feminists? What did radical feminists advocate? What did "the personal is political" mean? How and why did the boundaries between radical and mainstream feminists break down by the mid-1970s? (text, pp. 1050–1053; video segment 4)

18. Why and how was the relationship between feminism and ethnic minority women complicated? What were the common threads tying women together? How was American feminism connected to transnational feminism? (text, pp. 1049–1055; video segment 4)

19. What gains had women made by the mid-1970s? Why did an antifeminist movement arise? What other challenges did feminists face? (text, pp. 1052–1053; video segment 4)

20. Why and how did gay men and lesbians organize in the 1960s and 1970s? What were the results of their efforts? (text, pp. 1046–1048)

21. What characterized the environmental movement of the 1960s and 1970s? What role did Rachel Carson play? What were the results of this movement? What limited it? (text, pp. 1048–1049)

22. In summary, how and why did the student, American Indian, Latino, and feminist movements of this era transform America? How were freedom, equality, and identity expanded? What limited change? (text, all pages; video segments 2–5)

HISTORICAL EXPERTS INTERVIEWED

Albert Camarillo, Professor of History, Stanford University, Stanford, CA
Dorothy Sue Cobble, Professor of History and Labor Studies, Rutgers University, New Brunswick, NJ
Donald Fixico, Thomas Bowler Distinguished Professor of American Indian History, University of Kansas, Lawrence, KS
Todd Gitlin, Professor of History, Columbia University, New York, NY
Susan Hartmann, Professor of History, Ohio State University, Columbus, OH
Dolores Huerta, Founder, Dolores Huerta Foundation, Bakersfield, CA
Michael Kazin, Professor of History, Georgetown University, Washington, DC
Guadalupe San Miguel, Jr., Professor of History, University of Houston, Houston, TX
Gloria Steinem, Journalist and Founder, Ms. Foundation for Women, New York, NY

FEATURED FAMILY MEMBERS INTERVIEWED

Edward Archuleta, Santa Fe, NM
Philip Deloria, Ann Arbor, MI
Vine Deloria, Jr., Golden, CO
Charlene McAden, Blooming Grove, TX
Sherrie Tarpley, Melissa, TX
Dianne Swann-Wright, Lake Monticello, VA
Judy Yung, Santa Cruz, CA

PRACTICE TEST

The following items will help you evaluate your understanding of this lesson. Use the Answer Key at the end of the lesson to check your answers or to locate material related to each question.

Multiple Choice: Select the best answer.

1. The significance of the Port Huron Statement lay mainly in its _____.
   A. tone of urgent moral passion
   B. programs to bring about change
   C. opposition to the Vietnam War
   D. endorsement of bureaucratic institutions

2. Drawing on the example of the Beats of the 1950s, the counterculture of the 1960s _____.
   A. revered the writings of Emily Brontë
   B. focused on personal rather than political change
   C. insisted that the ends justified their violent means
   D. believed that a citizen's first responsibility was to society

3. An important goal of the American Indian Movement was _____.
   A. the establishment of "survival schools" to teach Indian history and values
   B. a return to the policies of relocation and termination
   C. full assimilation into mainstream America
   D. an end to traditional Native American religious practices

4. Vine Deloria and his book, *Custer Died for Your Sins*, were important because they _____.
   A. provided plans for Indian occupation of Little Big Horn
   B. articulated an Indian perspective on pressing issues
   C. emphasized the similarities of African Americans and American Indians
   D. advocated the repeal of all Indian treaties

5. Cesar Chavez and Dolores Huerta are best known for their efforts to _____.
   A. improve the conditions of migrant farmworkers in California
   B. demand that public schools teach a course in Mexican history
   C. ease restrictions on immigrants from Mexico
   D. fight for higher wages for factory workers

6. All of the following were results of Latino protests in the 1960s and 1970s EXCEPT _____.
   A. greater respect for their culture
   B. better enforcement of antidiscrimination laws
   C. sharp reduction in poverty
   D. more political office-holding

7. One factor underlying the new wave of feminism in the late 1960s and early 1970s was the _____.
   A. wholesale abandonment of the workplace by women after World War II
   B. declining number of women attending institutions of higher education
   C. the federal government's efforts to challenge women's traditional roles
   D. escalating number of women in the workplace

8. In the video "Times Are A-Changin'," the story of Charlene McAden and Sherrie McAden Tarpley illustrates _____.
   A. discrimination aimed at ethnic minority women
   B. lack of educational opportunities for women
   C. the application of Title IX of the Education Act
   D. the importance of birth control in women's lives

9. Women of color were critical of white women's organizations because those organizations _____.
   A. seemed indifferent to the poverty disproportionately faced by minority women
   B. largely focused on achieving voting rights for women
   C. seemed indifferent to the problems of women in the workplace
   D. failed to support women who were running for office

Short Answer: Your answer should respond to the points indicated in one or two paragraphs.

10. How did the American Indian and Chicano movements of the 1960s and early 1970s change their respective cultural identities?

11. How radical was "radical feminism"? What were its consequences?

Essay Question: Your response should be several paragraphs long and demonstrate a clear understanding of the points indicated.

12. How and why did the student, American Indian, Latino, and feminist movements of the 1960s and early 1970s transform America? How were American freedom, equality, and identity expanded? What limited change?

ANSWER KEY

	Answer	Learning Objectives	Focus Points	References
1.	A	LO 1	FP 1	Text, pp. 1042–1043; video segment 2
2.	B	LO 1	FP 4	Text, pp. 1043–1046; video segment 2
3.	A	LO 2	FP 6	Text, pp. 1039–1041; video segment 3
4.	B	LO 2	FP 8	video segment 3
5.	A	LO 3	FP 10	Text, pp. 1041–1042; video segment 3
6.	C	LO 3	FP 11	Text, pp. 1041–1042; video segment 3
7.	D	LO 4	FP 12	Text, pp. 1049–1050; video segment 4
8.	D	LO 4	FP 12	Video segment 4
9.	A	LO 4	FP 18	Text, pp. 1049–1055; video segment 4

10. .... LO 2, 3 .... FP 7, 11 .... Text, pp. 1040–1042; video segment
 - How did they change the way they thought about themselves?
 - How did they change the way others viewed them?
 - How was the expression of their cultural identities changed?

11. .... LO 4 .... FP 17 .... Text, pp. 1050–1053; video segment 4
 - What does the term "radical" mean?
 - What core issues did radical feminists address?
 - What aspects of women's lives changed?

12. .... LO 5 .... FP 22 .... Text, all pages; video segments 2–5
 - Consider the limitations faced by people in these respective movements.
 - How did they bring about change? Why was direct action used?
 - How were laws and institutions changed? How were courts influenced?
 - How were attitudes toward and expression of cultural values changed?
 - How was the meaning of being an American changed?
 - How did the movements move America closer to its founding principles?
 - How could identity politics limit change?

ENRICHMENT IDEAS

These activities are not required unless your instructor assigns them. They are offered as suggestions to help you learn more about the material presented in this lesson.

1. Interview someone who was active in the student, American Indian, Latino, or feminist movement of the 1960s and 1970s. Using the interview as a primary source and reflecting upon what you have learned in this lesson, write a well-developed essay in which you analyze how one of these movements brought about change in America.

2. If your parents or grandparents have personal experiences dating back to the 1960s and 1970s, interview one or both of them about how the social and cultural movements of the time affected their lives. Using that as a primary source to supplement what you have learned in this lesson, write a thoughtful essay in which you analyze how that era affected your family and American society in general.

3. Read the "Documenting The American Promise" feature on "Student Protest" on pages 1044–1045 of the text. Then submit an essay in which you thoroughly answer the questions posed in the text.

SUGGESTED READINGS/RESOURCES

See the "Bibliography" on pages 1058–1059 of the text if you wish to examine other books and resources related to material discussed in this lesson.

Lesson 19

The Vietnam Dilemma

OVERVIEW

On a cold January 20, 1961, President John F. Kennedy delivered a stirring inaugural address. He left no doubt about the commitment of the United States to continue to protect the frontiers of freedom: "Let every nation know, whether it wishes us well or ill, that we shall pay any price, bear any burden, meet any hardship, support any friend, oppose any foe . . . to assure the survival and the success of liberty."

Events in Cuba would soon test President Kennedy's resolve. The challenge of containing communism in the western hemisphere reached a critical and terrifying point in 1962 when the Cuban missile crisis brought the United States and the Soviet Union to the brink of nuclear war. Why did this happen? What was learned from this frightening experience?

The successful resolution of the Cuban missile crisis contributed to the willingness of the Kennedy administration to increase American involvement in an ongoing conflict in Vietnam. While we will never know what Kennedy ultimately would have done in Vietnam, we do know that President Lyndon B. Johnson authorized a major escalation of the war in 1965. As casualties mounted, so too did doubts about further prosecution of the war.

By 1968, President Johnson and the American people were ready to change course. The war was polarizing the nation, and Richard M. Nixon won the presidential election in part because he promised he had a plan to end the Vietnam War. President Nixon did proceed to de-escalate American ground forces, but the horrors of war continued until a ceasefire was arranged in 1973. Two years later, communist forces took over South Vietnam and reunited the country.

Indeed, the American people paid an enormous price and bore lasting burdens from a war that failed to achieve its objective. What did it all mean? How did the searing experiences of the Vietnam War transform America?

LESSON ASSIGNMENT

Text: Roark, et. al., *The American Promise*
- Chapter 29, "Vietnam and the Limits of Power," pp. 1063–1099

Video: "The Vietnam Dilemma," from the series *Transforming America*

LEARNING OBJECTIVES

This lesson examines how America grappled with dangerous issues in the world arena in the 1960s and early 1970s. Upon completion of this lesson, you should be able to:

1. Explain American foreign policy during the 1960s and early 1970s and the application of that policy in Cuba and throughout the world.

2. Explain why the United States became increasingly involved in Vietnam in the early 1950s and 1960s.

3. Analyze why the United States eventually withdrew from Vietnam.

4. Assess the legacy of the Vietnam War.

LESSON FOCUS POINTS

The following questions are designed to help you get the most benefit from the sources selected for this lesson. For reference purposes, the video is divided into five segments: (1) Introduction, (2) "A Fateful Miscalculation," (3) "Hey, Hey, LBJ!," (4) "Peace . . . with Honor?," and (5) Summary Analysis: "Vietnam Remains."

1. How and why did the Kennedy administration adjust American foreign policy and strategies in the early 1960s? How did this play out in the third world? What is important about the Peace Corps? (text, pp. 1063–1068)

2. Examine Map 29.1 on p. 1066 of the text. How would you answer the questions posed in the text? (text, p. 1066)

3. How and why did a missile crisis develop in Cuba by October 1962? What was at stake in this crisis? How was the crisis resolved? (text, pp. 1068–1069; video segment 1)

4. What were the consequences of the Cuban missile crisis? What lessons were learned? How is the missile crisis linked to what was going on in Vietnam? (text, p. 1069; video segment 2)

5. How and why did the United States get involved in Vietnam in the 1940s and 1950s? Why was the refusal to hold national elections in Vietnam in 1956 important? (text, p. 1070; video segment 2)

6. How did the Kennedy administration approach the situation in Vietnam? What actions did they take? Why was the situation complicated? (text, pp. 1070–1072; video segment 2)

7. How and why did President Lyndon Johnson and his administration initially address foreign policy issues and Vietnam as they did? What explains the Gulf of Tonkin Resolution? What was important about it? (text, pp. 1072–1073; video segment 2)

8. Why did President Johnson authorize a major escalation of the war in Vietnam in 1965? What were the consequences of this decision? Why did the Johnson administration make "a fateful miscalculation" about the war? (text, pp. 1072–1073; video segment 2)

9. What characterized the military operations in Vietnam? Who was fighting for the Americans on the ground? Why was the combat especially difficult? (text, pp. 1074–1081; video segment 2)

10. How and why did public opinion regarding the Vietnam War begin shifting in 1965? How was the antiwar movement expressing its opposition? Why was there initially a mixed reaction to the antiwar protesters? How and why did LBJ react as he did to the protest movement? (text, pp. 1078–1085; video segment 3)

11. Why did American involvement in the Vietnam War reach critical turning points in 1968? What was important about the Tet Offensive? Why was LBJ's address to the nation on March 31, 1968, important? How and why did antiwar protests intensify? How did the controversies surrounding the war affect the presidential election? (text, pp. 1082–1087; video segments 3, 4)

12. Why did President Richard Nixon and his top advisors reject a swift withdrawal from Vietnam? What were their objectives? How did they deal with the Soviet Union, China, and the third world? (text, pp. 1087–1090; video segment 4)

13. How did the Nixon administration propose to achieve "peace with honor" in Vietnam? What was the policy of "Vietnamization?" What problems were inherent in this policy? (text, p. 1090; video segment 4)

14. Why did President Nixon widen the war to Cambodia? What were the consequences of this action? What happened at Kent State and Jackson State in May 1970? Why were these incidents important? (text, pp. 1090–1091; video segment 4)

15. How were the troops in Vietnam between 1969 and 1973 affected by the developments in the war? Why did more veterans get involved in the antiwar movement at home? What effect did they have? How did revelations about My Lai and in the *Pentagon Papers* affect attitudes toward the war? (text, p. 1092; video segment 4)

16. Why were peace accords finally reached in January 1973? To what extent had "peace with honor" been achieved? What happened in Vietnam after American troops withdrew? (text, pp. 1093–1095; video segment 4)

17. In summary, how and why did the United States engage in the Vietnam War? What was the legacy of that war? What lessons were learned? How were the American people and the nation itself transformed by this experience? (text, all pages; video segments 2-5)

HISTORICAL EXPERTS INTERVIEWED

James Blight, Professor of International Relations, Watson Institute, Brown University, Providence, RI
William Broyles, Jr., Writer, Second Lieutenant, USMCR, Vietnam 1969-1970, Wilson, WY
George Herring, Professor of History, University of Kentucky, Lexington, KY
Michael Kazin, Professor of History, Georgetown University, Washington, DC
Bruce Schulman, Professor of History, Boston University, Boston, MA
Marilyn Young, Professor of History, New York University, New York, NY

FEATURED FAMILY MEMBERS INTERVIEWED

Bill Cecil, Jr., Asheville, NC
Bill Neebe, Wilmette, IL
Mark Neebe, Cambridge, MA

PRACTICE TEST

The following items will help you evaluate your understanding of this lesson. Use the Answer Key at the end of the lesson to check your answers or to locate material related to each question.

Multiple Choice: Choose the letter of the best answer.

1. The Peace Corps was launched by the Kennedy administration in 1961 to _____.
   A. quell domestic violence in America's major cities
   B. teach the leaders of third world countries about democracy
   C. work directly with the people in third world countries
   D. reduce the growing number of unemployed in the United States

2. The thirteen-day Cuban missile crisis of 1962 _____.
   A. brought the world's two superpowers perilously close to nuclear war
   B. followed the accidental firing of a missile at the U.S. Guantanamo naval base
   C. weakened President Kennedy's international standing
   D. ended with Fidel Castro's promise to hold democratic elections in Cuba

3. All of the following are lessons that can be derived from the Cuban Missile Crisis EXCEPT _____.
   A. nuclear war is possible
   B. nuclear weapons are inefficient in regional conflicts
   C. nuclear war can happen even though no one wants it
   D. nuclear weapons have to be abolished

4. The decision by the United States to support the cancellation of free elections in Vietnam in 1956 _____.
   A. was based on faulty intelligence reports
   B. violated one of America's democratic principles
   C. perpetuated French rule in the region
   D. led to an invasion by Chinese troops

5. The Gulf of Tonkin Resolution was important because it _____.
   A. illustrated inappropriate congressional oversight of presidential authority
   B. allowed Congress to withhold appropriations for military operations
   C. provided congressional authorization for escalation of forces in Vietnam
   D. required the president to have congressional approval before committing troops

6. The initiation of Operation Rolling Thunder in February 1965 was one sign that _____.
   A. the war in Vietnam had become America's war
   B. the war in Vietnam would soon end
   C. the French would be playing a larger role in the Vietnam conflict
   D. no additional U.S. troops would be needed in Vietnam

7. One of the practical reasons for protesting the Vietnam War was the belief that _____.
   A. the war could not be won
   B. no country has the right to interfere in the government of another
   C. the Vietnamese people had suffered unfairly
   D. the logic driving the Cold War was fundamentally unsound

8. The Tet Offensive marked a significant turning point in the Vietnam War because it _____.
   A. convinced Americans that more troops were needed
   B. illustrated that Nixon did not have a plan to win
   C. caused more people to question if the war could be won
   D. forced Americans to stop bombing North Vietnam

9. "Peace with honor" in Vietnam _____.
   A. ultimately meant billions of dollars in reparations to the North Vietnamese
   B. meant a truce that ended the direct involvement of the United States in the war
   C. resulted in the unconditional surrender of the North Vietnamese to American and South Vietnamese forces
   D. led to the reunification of Vietnam in April 1973

10. All of the following are lessons drawn from the Vietnam War EXCEPT _____.
    A. be cautious about sending troops into third world countries
    B. have clear objectives before going to war
    C. disseminate optimistic reports even when losing the conflict
    D. maintain strong public support at home for intervention overseas

Short Answer: Your answer should specifically address the points indicated in one or two paragraphs.

11. What are the main lessons derived from the Cuban Missile Crisis? How is that crisis linked to the Vietnam War?

12. Why and how did the United States get involved in Vietnam in the 1940s and 1950s? What was important about decisions made in that era?

13. Why did President Nixon pursue "peace with honor" in Vietnam? What were the results of this approach?

Essay Question: Your response should be several paragraphs long and elaborate on the points indicated in a manner that expresses understanding of the material.

14. How and why did the United States engage in the Vietnam War? Why did the U.S. forces leave Vietnam? What is the legacy of that war? How were the American people and the nation transformed by this experience?

ANSWER KEY

Answer	Learning Objectives	Focus Points	References
1. C	LO 1	FP 1	Text, pp. 1067–1068
2. A	LO 1	FP 3	Text, pp. 1068–1069; video segment 1
3. B	LO 1	FP 4	Text, p. 1069; video segments 1, 2
4. B	LO 2	FP 5	Video segment 2
5. C	LO 2	FP 7	Text, pp. 1072–1073; video segment 2
6. A	LO 2	FP 8	Text, pp. 1072–1073; video segment 2
7. A	LO 3	FP 10	Text, pp. 1077–1085; video segment 3
8. C	LO 3	FP 11	Text, p. 1083; video segment 3
9. B	LO 3	FP 13	Text, p. 1090; video segment 4
10. C	LO 4	FP 17	Text, pp. 1093–1096; video segment 5

11. .... LO 1, 2 .... FP 3, 4 .... Text, pp. 1068–1069; video segments 1, 2
    - Consider what could be learned about the danger of nuclear weapons.
    - What did the resolution of the crisis indicate about knowing your adversary?
    - Consider how attitudes and apprehensions carried over to Vietnam.

12. .... LO 2 .... FP 5 .... Video segment 2
    - Consider the Cold War and U.S. containment policy.
    - Why was aid given to the French? Why were the 1956 elections canceled?
    - How did these developments deepen the U.S. commitment?

13. .... LO 3 .... FP 13, 16 .... Text, pp. 1090–1095; video segment 4
    - Consider how this approach related to Nixon's larger agenda.
    - What happened during the four years leading up to peace accords?
    - What ultimately happened in Vietnam?

14. .... LO 2–4 .... FP 17 .... Text, all pages; video segments 2–5
    - Consider the containment policy and how Vietnam fit into that concept.
    - How did the decisions of the 1950s affect American commitment?
    - Why did President Johnson escalate the war? With what results?
    - Why and how did Johnson and President Nixon de-escalate the war?
    - How did the war affect people at home? Ultimately, why did the United States withdraw?
    - What was the cost of the war? How did the war affect soldiers and families?
    - What was learned about using American military power?
    - What were the consequences of the war? How was America transformed?

ENRICHMENT IDEAS

These activities are not required unless your instructor assigns them. They are offered as suggestions to help you learn more about the material presented in this lesson.

1. Interview a veteran of the Vietnam War or someone who expresses strong personal feelings about that war. Using that interview as a primary source and reflecting on what you have learned in this lesson, write a well-developed essay in which you analyze the effects of the Vietnam War on individuals, families, and the nation as a whole.

2. Investigate how the Vietnam War affected your local community and how the community commemorates that war. Then submit a thoughtful report on your findings, including your conclusions about legacy of the Vietnam War in your area.

3. Watch the documentary film, *The Fog of War*. Then submit a thoughtful review of that film and comment on the lessons stressed in the film.

SUGGESTED READINGS/RESOURCES

See the "Bibliography" on pages 1096–1097 of the text if you wish to examine other books and resources related to the material discussed in this lesson.

Lesson 20

The Decline of Liberalism

OVERVIEW

While the American people were experiencing the effects of the civil rights and other social movements at home and the consequences of pursuing containment in Vietnam, the national political winds were shifting. Liberalism was declining and political disillusionment was rising. Why was this happening? What did it mean?

The New Deal Political Coalition, which had basically dominated politics since the mid-1930s, was beginning to fall apart. We can trace this breakdown to the challenges presented to liberalism by the "New Left," President Lyndon Johnson's decisions to support minority civil and political rights, and the divisive effects of the Vietnam War. The 1968 presidential election illustrated the changes astir. With the Democrats in disarray, Republican Richard M. Nixon won the presidency.

Richard Nixon was a complex man who frequently sent mixed signals to the American people. He was the old cold warrior who sought détente with the Soviet Union and opened doors to communist China. On the domestic political front, he approved the extension of many liberal initiatives while appealing to a conservative base of supporters. Nixon won reelection in 1972 and spoke of less government in his second inaugural address in January 1973. Two days after that speech, Lyndon B. Johnson died. Liberalism appeared to be dying with him.

Strangely perhaps, it was President Nixon's corruption in office that put liberalism on life support. An incident during his successful reelection campaign led to the most serious constitutional crisis since the Civil War. Investigations of the Watergate Affair and other corrupt activities connected to the Nixon administration illustrated the need to limit the "imperial presidency." Nixon's resignation brought about an unusual transfer of power, but public cynicism toward government and politics intensified. As the United States celebrated its bicentennial, political currents swirling beneath the surface were pulling the American people in a different direction.

LESSON ASSIGNMENT

Text: Roark, et. al., *The American Promise*
- Chapter 28, "Reform, Rebellion, and Reaction," pp. 1048–1049, 1053, 1056–1058
- Chapter 29, "Vietnam and the Limits of Power," pp. 1082–1087
- Chapter 30, "America Moves to the Right," pp. 1101–1112

Video: "The Decline of Liberalism," from the series *Transforming America*

LEARNING OBJECTIVES

This lesson examines why liberalism declined as the major political philosophy in American public affairs. Upon completion of this lesson, you should be able to:

1. Analyze the presidential election of 1968.

2. Explain the domestic priorities and policies of the Nixon administration.

3. Analyze the development, exposure, and effects of the Watergate scandal.

4. Explain the decline of liberalism during the late 1960s and 1970s.

LESSON FOCUS POINTS

The following questions are designed to help you get the most benefit from the sources selected for this lesson. For reference purposes, the video is divided into five segments: (1) Introduction, (2) "Days of Hope, Days of Rage," (3) "A New Nixon?" (4) "The Imperial Presidency," and (5) Summary Analysis: "Beneath the Surface."

1. What is the essence of liberalism? (video introduction)

2. What was the key component of New Deal liberalism? How did liberalism evolve after World War II? Why was Lyndon B. Johnson's emergence as the principal champion of liberalism important? (video segment 2)

3. Why were the Democrats in disarray as they approached their presidential nominating convention in 1968? How did the events at the Chicago convention reflect political and national discord? (text, pp. 1082–1087; video segment 2)

4. Why was the 1968 presidential election significant? What was the "southern strategy" of the Republicans? Why was George Wallace an important political figure at this time? Why did Richard Nixon win? (text, pp. 1086–1087; video segment 2)

5. How and why did President Nixon carry out liberal reforms during his presidency? How and why did he put a conservative spin on these efforts? (text, pp. 1053, 1056–1058; video segment 3)

6. How and why did environmentalists have success in expanding their agenda in the late 1960s and early 1970s? What were the results of their efforts? (text, pp. 1048–1049; video segment 3)

7. How did President Nixon approach the major economic issues of his presidency? (text, pp. 1053, 1056–1058)

8. How did President Nixon court conservatives during his tenure in office? (text, pp. 1106–1108; video segment 3)

9. What were the most notable political developments during the 1972 presidential election? Why did Richard Nixon win? (text, pp. 1108–1109)

10. What does the term "imperial presidency" mean? What political dangers does the term imply? (text, p. 1109; video segment 4)

11. Why did the Watergate break-in turn into a major political scandal? Who was investigating the misdeeds associated with the Nixon administration? What constitutional issues were debated in the investigations? How was Nixon dealing with the investigations? (text, pp. 1109–1110; video segment 4)

12. On what grounds did the House Judiciary Committee recommend the impeachment of Richard Nixon? Why did Nixon resign? (text, p. 1110; video segment 4)

13. In the end, what did the Watergate Affair illustrate? What meaning did it have? How did the American people react? (video, segment 4)

14. What were the political results of the Watergate and other investigations of government operations at that time? (text, pp. 1110–1112)

15. Why did Gerald Ford lose the 1976 presidential election? Why did Jimmy Carter win? (text, pp. 1111–1112)

16. In summary, why and how did liberalism decline from the mid-1960s to the mid-1970s? What was important about this development? (text, all pages; video, segments 1–5)

HISTORICAL EXPERTS INTERVIEWED

Karl Brooks, Assistant Professor of History, University of Kansas, Lawrence, KS
Dan Carter, Educational/Foundation Professor, University of South Carolina, Columbia, NC
Archibald Cox, Professor of Law, Harvard Law School, Cambridge, MA
Joan Hoff, Research Professor of History, Montana State University, Bozeman, MT
Lisa McGirr, Dunwalke Associate Professor, Harvard University, Cambridge, MA
Bruce Schulman, Professor of History, Boston University, Boston, MA

FEATURED FAMILY MEMBERS INTERVIEWED

Vine Deloria, Jr., Golden, CO
Charlene McAden, Blooming Grove, TX
Judy Yung, Santa Cruz, CA

PRACTICE TEST

The following items will help you evaluate your understanding of this lesson. Use the Answer Key at the end of the lesson to check your answers or to locate material related to each question.

Multiple Choice: Choose the letter of the best answer.

1. After World War II, liberalism became _____.
    A. widely accepted among southern Democrats
    B. more concerned with social justice
    C. too closely allied with communism
    D. less popular in the northeastern United States

2. The turmoil surrounding the 1968 Democrat Party convention in Chicago _____.
    A. was instigated by Republican Party operatives
    B. convinced President Johnson not to seek reelection
    C. enabled George C. Wallace to get the party's nomination for president
    D. reflected the discord within the party and the nation

3. The presidential candidacy of George C. Wallace in 1968 appealed to _____.
    A. both civil rights and antiwar activists
    B. New Englanders in particular
    C. Americans who were outraged by assaults on traditional values by students and others
    D. black southerners who believed that the War on Poverty had stigmatized them

4. The U.S. president who created the Environmental Protective Agency was _____.
    A. John F. Kennedy
    B. Lyndon Baines Johnson
    C. Richard M. Nixon
    D. Jimmy Carter

5. During the Nixon administration, the number of government assistance programs _____.
    A. was reduced drastically
    B. did not change
    C. actually grew
    D. earned the growing support of conservatives

6. President Nixon saw Chief Justice Earl Warren's resignation in 1969 as an opportunity to put a _____.
    A. more liberal justice on the Court
    B. more conservative justice on the Court
    C. black justice on the Court
    D. conservative female justice on the Court

7. During the investigation of the Watergate Affair, one of the major constitutional questions was whether _____.
   A. Congress could impeach a sitting president
   B. the president could legally resign
   C. Congress could fire the special prosecutor named by the president
   D. the president is subject to the judicial process

8. The House Judiciary Committee voted to charge President Nixon with all of the following as grounds for impeachment EXCEPT _____.
   A. tax evasion
   B. abuse of power
   C. obstruction of justice
   D. contempt of Congress

9. A key factor in the disintegration of the liberal coalition was its _____.
   A. support for civil rights
   B. opposition to the Vietnam War
   C. endorsement of national liberation movements overseas
   D. lack of commitment to social justice issues

Short Answer: Your answer should specifically address the points indicated in one or two paragraphs.

10. How did the 1968 presidential election indicate that liberalism was facing decline?

11. Why can President Richard M. Nixon be considered the last of the liberal and the first of the conservative presidents in post-1960s America?

12. How and why did environmentalists expand their agenda in the 1960s and 1970s? What were the results of their efforts?

13. What constitutional questions were raised by President Nixon's Oval Office tapes? How did the tapes contribute to his decision to resign?

Essay Question: Your response should be several paragraphs long. Your answer should elaborate on the points indicated in a manner that expresses understanding of the material.

14. Why and how did liberalism decline from the mid-1960s to the mid-1970s? What was important about this development?

ANSWER KEY

	Answer	Learning Objectives	Focus Points	References
1.	B	LO 4	FP 2	Video segment 2
2.	D	LO 1	FP 3	Text, pp. 1086–1087; video segment 2
3.	C	LO 1	FP 4	Text, pp. 1086–1087; video segment 2
4.	C	LO 2	FP 6	Text, p. 1049
5.	C	LO 2	FP 5	Text, pp. 1053, 1056–1058; video segment 3
6.	B	LO 2	FP 8	Text, p. 1107
7.	D	LO 3	FP 11	Text, pp. 1109–1110; video segment 4
8.	A	LO 3	FP 12	Text, p. 1110
9.	A	LO 4	FP 16	Video segment 5

10. .... LO 1 .... FP 4 .... Text, pp. 1086–1087; video segment 2
    - Consider the growing anti-war protests and the domestic disturbances at the time.
    - What splits were showing up in the New Deal Political Coalition?
    - What were the results of the election?

11. .... LO 2 .... FP 5 .... Text, pp. 1053, 1056–1058; video segment 3
    - How did Nixon extend the liberal initiatives of the Great Society?
    - How did Nixon court the conservatives in America?

12. .... LO 2 .... FP 6 .... Text, pp. 1048–1049; video segment 3
    - What issues did environmentalist take on at this time?
    - What major pieces of legislation were passed?
    - Why did President Nixon endorse environmentalism?

13. .... LO 3 .... FP 11, 12 .... Text, pp. 1109–1110; video segment 4
    - Consider the checks and balances system in the federal government.
    - Does the president have special "executive privileges?"
    - How did the tapes implicate the president in the cover-up?

14. .... LO 5 .... FP 16 .... Text, all pages; video segments 1–5
    - What upheavals were apparent in American society by 1968? Who was being held responsible for the discord?
    - How did the 1968 presidential election indicate liberalism was weakening?
    - How did the Nixon administration appeal to conservatives?
    - How did the Watergate Affair affect liberalism?
    - How would the decline of liberalism shift the focus of domestic politics? Who would gain? Who would lose?

ENRICHMENT IDEAS

These activities are not required unless your instructor assigns them. They are offered as suggestions to help you learn more about the material presented in this lesson.

1. In a well-developed essay, compare and contrast the scandals of the U.S. Grant, Warren Harding, and Richard Nixon administrations. What are the lessons of these scandals?

2. Read *The Final Days* by Bob Woodward and Carl Bernstein and then write a critical analysis of it.

3. View the film *All the President's Men* and then submit a thoughtful report on what you learned from it.

4. Investigate the political philosophy and voting record of your representative in your state legislature or U.S. House of Representatives. Then submit a report in which you explain why this politician is a liberal or conservative.

SUGGESTED READINGS/RESOURCES

See the "Bibliography" on pages 1058–1059, 1096–1097, and 1136–1137 if you wish to examine other books and resources related to the material discussed in this lesson.

Unit III: Fiction and Film

Recommended novels and films set in the decades from World War II to Watergate:

On the Beach, by Nevil Shute. After a nuclear war, radiation slowly drifts toward the southern hemisphere. Australians and a few American refugees seek to maintain their daily lives, as the deadly rain moves ever closer and the world as we know it winds toward an inevitable end.

The Spy Who Came in from the Cold, by John LeCarré. In this intricately plotted tale of a British double agent who longs to end his career, LeCarré delves into the moral no-man's land of early Cold War Berlin. Widely considered to be the best spy story ever written.

On the Road, by Jack Kerouac. This cross-country bohemian odyssey captures the heart and soul of the Beat movement of the 1950s. Poetic, open and raw, Kerouac's prose penetrates into the deepest levels of American thought and culture.

The Women's Room, by Marilyn French. The classic feminist novel that awakened both women and men speaks to everyone about the deep feelings at the heart of love and relationships. A biting social commentary of an emotional world gone silently haywire.

All the President's Men, by Carl Bernstein and Bob Woodward. In the biggest political detective story of the century, two Washington Post reporters deliver the stunning revelations and pieces in the Watergate puzzle that brought about Nixon's downfall. A real life page-turner.

American Graffiti, d. George Lucas. This is not only a great movie, but a brilliant work of historical fiction. Complete with hot-rodders, teeny-boppers and an unforgettable soundtrack, it seems to recreate exactly how it was to be alive at that cultural instant, the summer of 1962.

Dr. Strangelove, or How I Learned to Stop Worrying and Love the Bomb, d. Stanley Kubrick. The ultimate satire of the nuclear age, Kubrick's Cold War classic is a perfect spoof of military and political insanity.

A Raisin in the Sun, d. Daniel Petrie. Adapted from the groundbreaking Broadway play, this film is a penetrating study of the personalities and conflicts within a working-class black family that is attempting to move into a white neighborhood in Chicago.

Four Little Girls, d. Spike Lee. A searing documentary by one of America's leading African American filmmakers concerning the 1963 bombing of the Sixteenth Street Baptist Church.

Incident at Oglala, d. Michael Apted. This eye-opening documentary is about Leonard Peltier, an AIM leader still in prison for the 1975 murder of two FBI agents. It presents compelling evidence of Peltier's innocence, and the possible political motivation for his conviction.

Apocalypse Now, d. Francis Ford Coppola. This Vietnam War epic follows a battle-weary Captain Willard on a secret upriver mission to find and execute the renegade Colonel Kurtz, who has reverted to a state of murderous and mystical insanity.

Unit IV

Reshaping America
1976–Present
"Still the Promised Land?"

21. Conservative Resurgence
22. A New Economy
23. Life in the Fast Lane
24. A Different World
25. Globalizing America
26. A More Perfect Union

THEME

The bicentennial of the United States provided an occasion for the American people to celebrate and to reflect. The principles of liberty and equality, proclaimed to all in the Declaration of Independence, remained at the core of the American promise. During the 1960s, the definitions of freedom and equality had been expanded to be more inclusive. While this was cause for celebration, more reflective Americans understood the challenges still present both at home and abroad. Recent developments had created new doubts about America's political leadership and the nation's ability to contain communism everywhere in the world.

As before, the process of transforming America continued in recent times. Politically, the pendulum initially moved right, gravitated back toward the center, and then swung right again. Economically, periods of boom and bust left many Americans uneasy. Socially, the face of America changed with a new surge of immigrants. Diversity of all kinds enriched the American experience and reminded all of the nation's promise. The end of the Cold War left the United States triumphant, but the world seemed more complex than ever. Terrorist attacks on America on September 11, 2001, shocked and unified the American people. Unfortunately, the conduct of a subsequent "war on terrorism" helped polarize the nation.

America has always been a resilient nation. American identity will continue to transform. The goals of freedom and equality are still there, but they remain contested. Throughout its history, the American people have been challenged to live up to the nation's promises and to form "a more perfect union." The challenge remains for Americans today.

Lesson 21

Conservative Resurgence

OVERVIEW

For this course, America's bicentennial in 1976 provides an opportunity to consider where the nation stood at that time on the themes of identity, freedom, and equality. "Americanism," as well as identity politics and culture, had expanded very dramatically in the preceding years. The goals of freedom and equality seemed more attainable for more people, but, as before, they remained contested territory.

It was not readily apparent in 1976, but conservatives were poised for a political resurgence. Liberalism was declining, and an energy crisis at home and perceived weakness abroad created a political opening. The proposed Equal Rights Amendment had moved social conservatives to become more politically active, and they united with economic conservatives to elect Ronald Reagan president in 1980.

Reagan's victory may have shocked liberals, but, in hindsight, it is quite understandable why he won. During his campaign, he had cleverly appealed to fears and hopes, and in his Inaugural Address he simply summarized the nation's problem as being "the government." The subsequent political changes are often referred to as the "Reagan Revolution." What did this mean? Why was it important?

Democrats may have been on the defensive during the 1980s, but Bill Clinton led the party to victories in the 1992 and 1996 presidential elections. However, Clinton was a "new" Democrat, and national politics continued on a conservative path, particularly after Republicans gained control of Congress in 1994. Clinton's personal conduct led to his impeachment by determined Republican opponents in 1998. While Clinton survived his trial in the Senate, his party was thrown on the defensive once again.

The controversial presidential election of 2000 ended with conservative Republican George W. Bush being inaugurated in 2001. Nevertheless, big government was likely here to stay. But whom would it serve?

LESSON ASSIGNMENT

Please Note: Chapters 30 and 31 in the text provide information relative to lessons 21-25 in this course. It is recommended that you read those two chapters in their entirety to get an overview and then return to the text to reread the specific assignments indicated for each lesson.

Text: Roark, et. al., *The American Promise*
- Chapter 30, "America Moves to the Right," pp. 1100–1108, 1111–1116, 1119–1128, 1136–1139
- Chapter 31, "The End of the Cold War and the Challenges of Globalization," pp. 1143–1146, 1151–1156, 1167–1171, 1175–1179

Video: "Conservative Resurgence," from the series *Transforming America*

LEARNING OBJECTIVES

This lesson analyzes the course themes in 1976 and then examines the major political developments since that time. Upon completion of this lesson, you should be able to:

1. Assess the status of American identity, freedom, and equality in 1976.

2. Explain the development and growth of the conservative movement in the 1960s and 1970s.

3. Analyze the presidential election of 1980 and the political legacy of President Ronald Reagan.

4. Analyze the politics of the 1990s, the legacy of President Bill Clinton, and the results of the 2000 presidential election.

5. Assess the political state of the nation in the early 2000s.

LESSON FOCUS POINTS

The following questions are designed to help you get the most benefit from the sources selected for this lesson. For reference purposes, the video is divided into five segments:
(1) Introduction/Unit IV Open, (2) "The Rise of the Right," (3) "The Reagan Revolution," (4) "Aiming for the Middle," and (5) Summary Analysis: "Here to Stay."

1. How and why had the definition of Americanism changed during the period of 1945-1976? Why had identity politics and culture taken on new meanings? What were the effects of these changes? (video segment 1)

2. By the mid-1970s, how and why had the meanings of freedom and equality changed? How were these concepts being contested in society? (video segment 1)

3. What factors explain the emergence of a grassroots conservative movement in the 1960s and early 1970s? What issues concerned conservatives? What role did Phyllis Schlafly play in this movement? (text, pp. 1101–1106; video segment 2)

4. How and why did the proposed Equal Rights Amendment galvanize the social and religious conservatives? How did Phyllis Schlafly and the Stop ERA organization proceed to block ratification of the proposed amendment? (text, pp. 1101–1102, 1122–1123; video segment 2)

5. In the end, why did the ERA fail? What was important about its defeat? How did all of the controversy about ERA affect the conservative movement as a whole? (text, pp. 1122–1123, 1128; video segment 2)

6. Why and how did President Jimmy Carter retreat from liberalism and experience political difficulties during his tenure in office? How did the Carter administration deal with energy and environmental issues? (text, pp. 1112–1116; video segment 3)

7. What strengths did Ronald Reagan have in the 1980 presidential election? Why did he win the election? What did his victory represent? (text, pp. 1100, 1119–1121; video segment 3)

8. What issues and policies did President Reagan promote? What were the political effects of his presidency? What is the meaning of the "Reagan Revolution?" (text, pp. 1121, 1124–1129, 1136; video segment 3)

9. Why had the word "liberal" become a dirty word by the 1980s? (video segment 4)

10. How did President George H. W. Bush further the conservative agenda? In what ways did he demonstrate a "kinder, gentler" approach? (text, pp. 1143–1146)

11. Why was Bill Clinton considered a "new" Democrat? What did that mean? Why did Clinton win the 1992 presidential election? (text, pp. 1151–1152; video segment 4)

12. What issues did President Clinton address early in his presidency? What success did he have? How did he change the face of government? (text, pp. 1152–1154; video segment 4)

13. Why did President Clinton pursue centrist policies, particularly after 1994? How did he bow to conservatives on homosexual issues? Why and how was the welfare system reformed? (text, pp. 1154–1155; video segment 4)

14. Why was President Clinton impeached? Why did he survive the impeachment trial in the Senate? In the end, what was Clinton's most significant accomplishment? (text, 1154–1157; video segment 4)

15. Why did George W. Bush win the 2000 presidential election? How did President George W. Bush address major domestic issues? (text, pp. 1167–1171; video segment 4)

16. In summary, why and how did a conservative resurgence take place in American politics since 1976? What effects did this resurgence have on American politics and the role of the federal government in American life? (text, all pages; video segments 1–5)

HISTORICAL EXPERTS INTERVIEWED

Albert Camarillo, Professor of History, Stanford University, Stanford, CA
Clayborne Carson, Professor of History and Editor of Martin Luther King, Jr. Papers, Stanford University, Stanford, CA
Dan Carter, Educational/Foundation Professor, University of South Carolina, Columbia, NC
William Chafe, Professor of History, Duke University, Chapel Hill, NC
Eric Foner, Professor of History, Columbia University, New York, NY
David Gutierrez, Professor of History, University of California, San Diego, CA
Susan Hartmann, Professor of History, Ohio State University, Columbus, OH
Alice Kessler-Harris, Professor of History, Columbia University, New York, NY
Lisa McGirr, Dunwalke Associate Professor, Harvard University, Cambridge, MA
Phyllis Schlafly, President, Eagle Forum, St. Louis, MO
Gloria Steinem, Journalist and Founder, Ms. Foundation for Women, New York, NY

FEATURED FAMILY MEMBERS INTERVIEWED

Bill Cecil, Jr., Asheville, NC
Harry Dingenthal, Garland, TX

PRACTICE TEST

The following items will help you evaluate your understanding of this lesson. Use the Answer Key at the end of the lesson to check your answers or to locate material related to each question.

Multiple Choice: Choose the letter of the best answer.

1. During the period of 1945-1976, American ethnic, racial, and gender minority groups _____.
   A. achieved parity in corporate leadership positions
   B. saw the benefit of expressing self-identity
   C. lost ground on the issue of free speech
   D. faced increasing restriction on access to education

2. In her 1964 book, *A Choice Not an Echo*, Phyllis Schlafly _____.
   A. praised the Republican party for its moderate views and policies
   B. praised the liberal elite Eastern establishment
   C. called for the easing of Cold War tensions
   D. pushed Barry Goldwater for president

3. Supporters of the proposed Equal Rights Amendment (ERA) _____.
   A. denigrated the role of housewife
   B. wanted to force women into combat
   C. underestimated those opposed to its ratification
   D. represented only a small percentage of Americans

4. The election of 1980 was significant because _____.
   A. it signaled a resurgence of support for the Great Society
   B. conservatives had begun to lose their dominance of the Republican Party
   C. conservatives had come to dominate the Republican Party
   D. voter turnout was the highest it had been since 1964

5. Ronald Reagan earned the nickname the "Teflon President" because _____.
   A. none of his mistakes or falsehoods seemed to stick to him
   B. of his tough stance against the Soviet Union
   C. he was a strong supporter of the cookware industry
   D. he survived an assassination attempt in March 1981

6. The word "liberal" became a dirty word in the 1980s because _____.
   A. conservatives provided the definition of the term
   B. liberals supported drug use and prostitution
   C. conservatives successfully balanced the budget
   D. liberals stopped believing in equal rights

7. President George H. W. Bush saw himself as a guardian of the Reagan legacy, but he was more inclined than President Reagan had been to _____.
   A. veto environmental legislation
   B. lift restrictions on abortion
   C. approve government activity in the private sphere
   D. separate government and the private sphere

8. Bill Clinton won the 1992 presidential election for all of the following reasons EXCEPT _____.
   A. his skills as a campaigner
   B. Ross Perot dropped out of the race
   C. the economy went into a slump
   D. George H.W. Bush's weaknesses

9. The welfare reform measures passed during the Clinton presidency _____.
   A. abolished traditional welfare programs
   B. were diametrically opposed to the welfare measures favored by Republicans
   C. strengthened the Aid to Families with Dependent Children program
   D. set a lifetime limit on welfare payments of five years

10. In 1998, the House of Representatives voted to impeach President Clinton on the _____.
    A. counts of perjury and obstruction of justice
    B. grounds of his having had sexual relations with a White House intern
    C. basis of his links to a phony real estate deal in Mississippi
    D. grounds of his alleged sexual harassment of an Arkansas state worker

Short Answer: Your answer should specifically address the points indicated in one or two paragraphs.

11. How and why did the meaning of American identity change between 1945-1976?

12. Why were the debates over the ratification of the proposed Equal Rights Amendment important to the conservative movement?

13. Why was President Bill Clinton impeached? Why did he survive his Senate trial on charges brought against him?

Essay Question: Your response should be several paragraphs long. Your answer should elaborate on the points indicated in a manner that expresses understanding of the material.

14. Why and how did a conservative resurgence take place in American politics since 1976? What effects did this resurgence have on American politics and the role of the federal government in American life?

ANSWER KEY

	Answer	Learning Objectives	Focus Points	References
1.	B	LO 1	FP 1	Video segment 1
2.	D	LO 2	FP 3	Text, p. 1101
3.	C	LO 2	FP 4	Text, pp. 1101–1102, 1122–1123; video segment 2
4.	C	LO 3	FP 7	Text, pp. 1100, 1119–1121; video segment 3
5.	A	LO 3	FP 8	Text, p. 1121; video segment 3
6.	A	LO 3	FP 9	Video segment 4
7.	C	LO 3	FP 10	Text, p. 1143
8.	B	LO 4	FP 11	Text, pp. 1151–1152; video segment 4
9.	D	LO 4	FP 13	Text, pp. 1154–1155; video segment 4
10.	A	LO 4	FP 14	Text, pp. 1155–1156; video segment 4

11. .... LO 1 .... FP 1 .... Video segment 1
- Consider the ways in which the definition of being American changed.
- How did civil rights and immigration legislation affect identity?
- How did identity politics and expression of self identity change?

12. .... LO 2 .... FP 3, 4, 5 .... Text, pp. 1101–1106, 1122–1123, 1128
.... video segment 2
- Why and how did the ERA issue unite the conservatives?
- What tactics were used to defeat the ERA?
- How did this affect the 1980 presidential election?

13. .... LO 4 .... FP 14 .... Text, pp. 1155–1156; video segment 4
- What were the formal charges against Clinton?
- What other issues played a role in both the impeachment and trial?

14. .... LO 2–5 .... FP 16 .... Text, all pages, video segments 2–5
- Consider why more people were losing faith in the government in the 1970s.
- What role did the ERA issue play?
- How did Ronald Reagan engage in conservative politics? What was the "Reagan Revolution?"
- How did Bill Clinton represent a "new" Democrat? What did that mean?
- How did George W. Bush practice conservative politics?
- What did "conservative" and "liberal" mean by the early 2000s? How were political parties affected?
- To what extent did the role of the federal government change during this period?

ENRICHMENT IDEAS

These activities are not required unless your instructor assigns them. They are offered as suggestions to help you learn more about the material presented in this lesson.

1. Interview at least three people who voted in the 1980 **or** the 2000 presidential election. Determine whom they voted for and their reasons for doing so. Then submit your findings in a well-developed essay in which you also present your observations about why people vote as they do.

2. In a thoughtful essay, compare and contrast the impeachment proceedings brought against Presidents Richard Nixon and Bill Clinton. What conclusions did you draw from your analysis?

3. Investigate the effects of third parties on the outcomes of the 1992 and 2000 presidential elections. Submit your findings and conclusions in a well-developed essay.

SUGGESTED READINGS/RESOURCES

See the "Bibliography" on pages 1136–1137 and 1176–1177 of the text if you wish to examine other books and resources related to the material discussed in this lesson.

Lesson 22

A New Economy

OVERVIEW

During the 1970s, the American economy was suffering from a malaise that analysts described as "stagflation." Slow growth, along with rising inflation, interest, and unemployment rates, led to an increasing frustration that was only compounded by an energy shortage. What was going on here? Why was this happening? What could be done to cure the economic ills?

During his successful presidential election campaign in 1980, Ronald Reagan presented a vision of a renewed America, a nation once again prosperous, powerful, and proud. He offered simple answers to complex economic policy questions. Once in office, he moved quickly to implement an updated version of the trickle-down economic policies used in the 1920s. Taxes were cut and business regulations were relaxed or removed. Huge increases in military spending helped spur an economic recovery, but it was being financed on credit.

One of the most significant developments of the late twentieth century was the diminishing strength of labor unions in America. Union-busting actions by government and corporations, de-industrialization, and outsourcing of jobs often left workers struggling to maintain their preferred standard of living. More women entered the work force, but wage gaps persisted.

Meanwhile, a "new economy" powered by the computer emerged in the 1990s. Entrepreneurs capitalized on new opportunities to provide new services. Good times appeared to have returned, but the bubble burst at the turn of the twenty-first century. Once again, Americans were looking for the ideal mix of public policy and private initiatives to restore their faith in the economic promise of America.

LESSON ASSIGNMENT

Text: Roark, et. al., *The American Promise*
- Chapter 30, "America Moves to the Right," pp. 1112–1116, 1121, 1124–1126, 1136–1139
- Chapter 31, "The End of the Cold War and the Challenges of Globalization," pp. 1143–1146, 1152–1157, 1160–1166, 1168–1171, 1175–1179

Video: "A New Economy," from the series *Transforming America*

LEARNING OBJECTIVES

This lesson examines the major economic developments of the last quarter of the twentieth century. Upon completing this lesson, you should be able to:

1. Examine the major economic issues facing the nation during this era.

2. Analyze the economic policies adopted by the federal government in this period.

3. Analyze the diminishing influence of unions and the changing nature of work.

4. Examine the costs and benefits of the "new economy" that emerged in the 1990s.

5. Assess the economic state of the nation at the beginning of the twenty-first century.

LESSON FOCUS POINTS

The following questions are designed to help you get the most benefit from the sources selected for this lesson. For reference purposes, the video is divided into five segments: (1) Introduction, (2) "Trickle Down," (3) "America at Work," (4) "The New Wave," and (5) Summary Analysis: "The Ideal Mix."

1. Why was the American economy in a slump in the mid and late 1970s? Why was there an energy crisis? How was the poor economy affecting the American people? (text, pp. 1112–1116; video segments 1, 2)

2. How did President Carter address the economic issues? What success did he have? What limited his success? (text, pp. 1112–1116; video segments 1, 2)

3. What is the basic belief of those who support the "trickle-down" or "supply-side" theory of economics? How is this different from "bubble-up" or Keynesian economics? (text, p. 1121; video segment 2)

4. How did the "Laffer Curve" help justify tax cuts? What were the results of the tax cuts of the Reagan administration? (text, p. 1121; video segment 2)

5. What were the advantages and disadvantages of government deregulation of business in the 1980s? How did the savings and loan crisis of the 1980s relate to deregulation? (text, pp. 1124–1125; video segment 2)

6. How did President Reagan deal with the air traffic controllers' (PATCO) strike in 1981? Why did he take those actions? What were the results? (text, p. 1124; video segment 3)

7. Why did so many companies "downsize" and/or "outsource" work in the 1980s and 1990s? What effect did this have on workers and the communities in which they lived? (text, pp. 1125–1127; video segment 3)

8. How did new technology affect work and the labor market? What is "de-industrialization?" (text, pp. 1125–1126; video segment 3)

9. How did women workers fare during this era? Why did a wage gap persist? What were the pros and cons of flexible work? (text, p. 1126; video segment 3)

10. By the end of the century, why did it appear that workers were less likely to rise above the economic class into which they were born? (text, pp. 1126, 1156–1157; video segment 3)

11. How did President George H. W. Bush and his administration approach economic issues? What were the results of their policies? (text, pp. 1143–1146)

12. How did President Clinton and his administrations deal with the economy? What were the effects of their policies? (text, pp. 1152–1157)

13. Why did a "new wave" of the service economy emerge in the 1990s? How did this differ from earlier waves of service sector employment? (video segment 4)

14. How and why did the development of the Internet change American and world economies in the 1990s? (text, pp. 1162–1163; video segment 4)

15. Why did a speculative bubble emerge around dot.com stocks in the 1990s? What caused the bubble to burst? (video segment 4)

16. What characterized the economic policies of the George W. Bush administration? (text, pp. 1168–1171)

17. In summary, what major changes took place in the American economy during the last quarter of the twentieth century? Why did these changes occur? What was the state of the economy by the year 2000? (text, all pages; video segments 1-5)

HISTORICAL EXPERTS INTERVIEWED

Kevin Boyle, Associate Professor, Ohio State University, Columbus, OH
Steve Cobb, Chairperson of Department of Economics, University of North Texas, Denton, TX
Dorothy Sue Cobble, Professor of History and Labor Studies, Rutgers University, New Brunswick, NJ
Nelson Lichtenstein, Professor of History, University of California, San Barbara, CA
Julianne Malveaux, Economist and Author, Last Wave Productions, Washington, DC

FEATURED FAMILY MEMBERS INTERVIEWED

Bill Cecil, Jr., Asheville, NC
Vine Deloria, Jr., Golden, CO
Bill Neebe, Wilmette, IL
Mark Neebe, Cambridge, MA
Judy Yung, Santa Cruz, CA

PRACTICE TEST

The following items will help you evaluate your understanding of this lesson. Use the Answer Key at the end of the lesson to check your answers or to locate material related to each question.

Multiple Choice: Choose the letter of the best answer.

1. The slumping economy of the late 1970s contributed to a national sense of _____.
   A. frustration
   B. sacrifice
   C. patriotism
   D. cooperation

2. In 1979, in response to the nation's dependence on foreign oil, President Carter established the _____.
   A. Department of Energy
   B. Department of Health and Human Services
   C. Energy Protection Agency
   D. Bureau of Energy Conservation

3. President Reagan's initial strategy to fix the lagging U.S. economy involved _____.
   A. lowering interest rates
   B. introducing a massive tax cut
   C. pumping federal money into the economy
   D. increasing taxes

4. In the video, "A New Economy," economist Julianne Malveaux makes the point that _____.
   A. federal deficits are not a long-term problem
   B. capitalism works more smoothly and fairly with oversight
   C. unions have outlived their usefulness
   D. corporate executives deserve their high salaries

5. During the 1980s and 1990s, the work force in America _____.
   A. became more segmented between low and high wage workers
   B. moved toward solidarity with European workers
   C. favored the removal of government regulations on industry
   D. had more opportunities for manufacturing jobs

6. One reason George H. W. Bush ultimately abandoned his no-new-taxes pledge was that he _____.
   A. had inherited a huge budget deficit from the Reagan administration
   B. came to believe that higher taxes would solidify his conservative base
   C. never intended to honor the pledge in the first place
   D. hoped to expand costly domestic programs

7. The Clinton administration ended its eight years in office with _____.
    A. a record deficit in the federal budget
    B. a surplus in the federal budget and the longest economic boom in history
    C. an abysmal record on women's rights, gay rights, and the environment
    D. a huge increase in spending on welfare programs

8. The "new wave" of the service economy of the 1980s and 1990s featured jobs in the area of _____.
    A. information technology
    B. government services
    C. retail sales
    D. financial services

Short Answer: Your answer should specifically address the points indicated in one or two paragraphs.

9. How does trickle-down/supply side economics differ from Keynesian/bubble-up economics? Who benefits most from each practice?

10. What were the advantages and disadvantages of the deregulation of business in the 1980s?

11. What explains the decline of unions in the 1980s and 1990s?

Essay Question: Your response should be several paragraphs long. Your answer should elaborate of the points indicated in a manner that expresses understanding of the material.

12. Explain the main features of the "new economy" that emerged in America in the 1980s and 1990s. How and why was this economy different from those of earlier eras? How was it similar? What economic challenges existed at the beginning of the twenty-first century?

ANSWER KEY

Answer	Learning Objectives	Focus Points	References
1. A	LO 1	FP 1	Text, pp. 1112–1116; video segments 1–2
2. A	LO 2	FP 2	Text, p. 1114
3. B	LO 2	FP 5	Text, pp. 1124–1125; video segment 2
4. B	LO 2	FP 5	Video segment 2
5. A	LO 3	FP 7, 8	Text, pp. 1125–1127; video segment 3
6. A	LO 2	FP 11	Text, p. 1146
7. B	LO 2, 4	FP 12	Text, pp. 1156–1157
8. A	LO 4	FP 13	Video segment 4

9. ....LO 2....................FP 3................................Text, p. 1121; video segment 2
   - Consider the role of government in each case.
   - What is the logic of each?
   - What tends to happen with income distribution?

10. ....LO 2....................FP 5...................................Text, pp. 1124–1125; video segment 2
    - What effect did deregulation have on corporate operations?
    - Who and/or what suffers from deregulation?

11. ....LO 3....................FP 6, 7, 8...........................Text, pp. 1124–1127; video segment 3
    - How did government policies and attitudes affect unions?
    - What effects did the changing nature of the work force have?
    - How did corporations make life difficult for unions?

12. ....LO 1–5..................FP 17......................................Text, all pages; video segments 1–5
    - Consider what sectors of the economy changed.
    - How did technology affect the economy?
    - Why and how did the work force change?
    - What role was the government playing?
    - How and why were corporations operating differently?
    - Compare and contrast briefly with previous eras covered in this course.
    - Who were the winners and losers in the new economy?
    - Identify the big issues remaining.

ENRICHMENT IDEAS

These activities are not required unless your instructor assigns them. They are offered as suggestions to help you learn more about the material presented in this lesson.

1. In a well-developed essay, compare and contrast the application of trickle-down economic policies in the 1920s, 1980s, and early 2000s. What conclusions did you draw from your analysis?

2. In a thoughtful position paper, take a stand on the regulation or deregulation of business in America as it affects the general welfare of the people. In your argument, be sure to acknowledge the points made by those who may hold a contrary opinion.

3. Investigate the status of organized labor in your area (city, county, region, or state). How and why has that status changed in the last thirty years? What effects have those changes had on working class families? Report your findings in a concise essay.

SUGGESTED READINGS/RESOURCES

See the "Bibliography" on pages 1136–1137 and 1176–1177 of the text if you wish to examine other books and resources related to the material discussed in this lesson.

Lesson 23

Life in the Fast Lane

OVERVIEW

Socially and culturally, American life in the late twentieth century was similar in some ways to the Gilded Age of a century earlier. The lifestyles of the rich and famous still grabbed public attention, and those at the lower end of the economic ladder still struggled to make ends meet. Contemporary Americans may have enjoyed more freedoms than their ancestors, but nagging social problems persisted. The pace of life had quickened, but why was everyone so busy? How and why was life in America changing? What did it all mean?

    One of the most obvious and significant social changes in recent America had to do with the very composition of the American people. Immigration levels near the end of the twentieth century were comparable to those of the huddled masses who entered the United States nearly a century before. However, these recent arrivals were largely coming from different parts of the world. Why were so many Asians and Latinos coming to America? How were they transforming America and American identity?

    Keeping alive the American dream of equality in such a diverse society continued to be a formidable challenge. "Affirmative action," a term used since the civil rights movement of the 1960s, took on new and sometimes divisive connotations. While some may have argued that equal rights and opportunities existed, it was clear that race, as well as ethnicity, gender, and sexual orientation, still mattered in America. After all these years, where were we on the equality question?

LESSON ASSIGNMENT

Text: Roark, et.al., *The American Promise*
- Chapter 30, "America Moves to the Right," pp. 1103–1108, 1114–1116, 1125–1132, 1136–1139
- Chapter 31, "The End of the Cold War and the Challenges of Globalization," pp. 1143–1146, 1152–1157, 1161, 1164–1171, 1176–1179

Video: "Life in the Fast Lane," from the series *Transforming America*

LEARNING OBJECTIVES

This lesson examines the major social and cultural developments in America during the last quarter of the twentieth century. Upon completing this lesson, you should be able to:

1. Analyze the development and consequences of the "culture of wealth" in the 1980s and 1990s.

2. Explain the major social issues of the era, including the exercise of personal freedom.

3. Analyze the causes and consequences of recent immigration to America.

4. Examine the state of race relations and the ongoing debates about affirmative action in America.

5. Assess the meaning of the major social developments of this era.

LESSON FOCUS POINTS

The following questions are designed to help you get the most benefit from the sources selected for this lesson. For reference purposes, the video is divided into five segments: (1) Introduction, (2) "Living in America," (3) "Immigration: The Next Generation," (4) "Race Matters," and (5) Summary Analysis: "Harder Than Rocket Science."

1. How was the "culture of wealth" promoted during the 1980s and 1990s? What were the consequences of the emphasis on materialism? (text, pp. 1125–1126; video segment 2)

2. Why and how did individual self-expression change in this period? Who were the "yuppies?" (text, pp. 1125–1126; video segment 2)

3. Why did the income gap widen during this era? How was poverty evident in America? How was the nation's welfare system reformed in 1996? (text, pp. 1125–1127, 1152–1155; video segment 1)

4. In what ways did women's lives change during the 1980s and 1990s? How did this affect the family? (text, pp. 1125–1128, 1153–1155; video segment 2)

5. Why did drug use and violence spread? How did people react to these conditions? (video segment 2)

6. Why and how did the gay and lesbian rights movement gain momentum during this era? What were the consequences of this movement? (text, pp. 1129–1132, 1154)

7. What were the major issues facing environmentalists in the late twentieth century? (text, pp. 1114–1116, 1124, 1143, 1152, 1161, 1169–1171)

8. How and why did the United States change its immigration policies in 1965? What were the consequences of this policy change? (text, pp. 1161, 1164–1167; video, segment 3)

9. In particular, how did recent immigration affect Latino, Asian, and other communities within the United States? What effect did this immigration have on American identity? (video segment 3)

10. What is "affirmative action?" Why is it controversial? What does this issue illustrate about America? (text, pp. 1107–1108; video segment 4)

11. Why were the affirmative action cases involving the University of Michigan important? What were the results of the cases? (video segment 4)

12. In general, how and why did American society change in the last quarter of the twentieth century? In particular, how and why did freedom, equality, and identity change in America? (text, all pages; video, all segments)

HISTORICAL EXPERTS INTERVIEWED

Christopher Edley, Dean, University of California Law School, Berkeley, CA
Nick Gillespie, Editor-in-Chief, *Reason Magazine*, Oxford, OH
Guadelupe San Miguel, Professor of History, University of Houston, Houston, TX
Susan Strasser, Professor of History, University of Delaware, Newark, DE
Judy Wu, Assistant Professor, Ohio State University, Columbus, OH

FEATURED FAMILY MEMBERS INTERVIEWED

Peg Burns, Ann Arbor, MI
Philip Deloria, Ann Arbor, MI
Charlene McAden, Blooming Grove, TX
Dianne Swann-Wright, Lake Monticello, VA
Ellen Wright, Charlottesville, VA
Judy Yung, Santa Cruz, CA

PRACTICE TEST

The following items will help you evaluate your understanding of this lesson. Use the Answer Key at the end of the lesson to check your answers or to locate material related to each question.

Multiple Choice: Choose the letter of the best answer.

1. The group that best symbolized Americans' celebration of wealth in the 1980s was the _____.
   A. Christian Coalition
   B. John Birch Society
   C. hippies
   D. yuppies

2. One of the major factors supporting the culture of wealth in the 1980s and 1990s was the _____.
   A. easy availability of credit
   B. popularity of the religious right
   C. development of the Internet
   D. narrowing of the income gap between rich and poor

3. During the 1980s, average personal income increased and economic inequality _____.
   A. increased as well
   B. decreased
   C. remained unchanged
   D. virtually disappeared

4. In the video, "Life in the Fast Lane," the Peg Burns-Philip Deloria family illustrates the _____.
   A. harshness of inner-city life
   B. continuation of the 1950s "Leave it to Beaver" lifestyle
   C. discrimination women face in the job market
   D. changing roles for women and men in the modern household

5. Advances in gay and lesbian rights in the 1970s and 1980s included _____.
   A. the American Psychiatric Association's decision to no longer categorize homosexuality as a mental illness
   B. several openly gay politicians winning elective office
   C. a number of cities banning job discrimination against homosexuals.
   D. all of the above

6. President Carter sponsored legislation to create the Superfund in response to the _____.
   A. environmental disaster in Love Canal, New York
   B. explosion of a nuclear reactor in Chernobyl, Ukraine
   C. AIDS crisis
   D. growing problem of stagflation

7. The fastest-growing immigrant groups in the United States at the end of the twentieth century were Latinos and _____.
   A. people from the former Soviet Union
   B. West Africans
   C. people from the Middle East
   D. Asians

8. In the video, "Life in the Fast Lane," affirmative action is described as a policy that _____.
   A. pays attention to race and gender in decision-making
   B. reverses the gains of the civil rights laws of the 1960s
   C. guarantees jobs for unqualified applicants
   D. explains why white men have lost status in America

Short Answer: Your answer should specifically address the points indicated in one or two paragraphs.

9. Why is dealing with race in America "harder than rocket science"?

10. How did immigration in the last quarter of the twentieth century affect American identity?

11. How did Americans express a greater degree of personal freedom in the 1980s and 1990s?

Essay Question: Your response should be several paragraphs long. Your answer should elaborate on the points indicated in a manner that expresses understanding of the material.

12. How and why did freedom, equality, and identity change in America during the last quarter of the twentieth century?

13. Compare and contrast American society in 1980-2000 with the American society that existed in the period 1880-1900. What explains the similarities and differences?

ANSWER KEY

	Answer	Learning Objectives	Focus Points	References
1.	D	LO 1	FP 2	Text, pp. 1125–1126; video segment 2
2.	A	LO 1	FP 1	Text, pp. 1125–1126; video segment 2
3.	A	LO 2	FP 3	Text, p. 1126, video segment 1
4.	D	LO 2	FP 4	video segment 2
5.	D	LO 2	FP 6	Text, pp. 1129–1132
6.	A	LO 2	FP 7	Text, pp. 1115–1116
7.	D	LO 3	FP 8	Text, pp. 1165–1167; video segment 3
8.	A	LO 4	FP 10	video segment 4

9. .... LO 4 .... FP 10 .... video segments 4, 5
   - Consider how race has been used in the past.
   - Why is affirmative action so controversial? What is at stake?
   - Why is the issue less predictable than science?

10. .... LO 3 .... FP 8, 9 .... Text, pp. 1164–1167; video segment 3
    - Where were most of the recent immigrants coming from?
    - How was this different from previous immigration?
    - How did this immigration affect ethnic identity?

11. .... LO 2 .... FP 2-6 .... video segment 2
    - What lifestyle options were open that previously did not exist?
    - How were women affected?
    - How was freedom connected to the consumer culture?

12. .... LO 5 .... FP 12 .... Text, all pages; video segments 1–5
    - In what ways did American pop culture celebrate freedom?
    - What new freedoms did women experience?
    - What were some of the challenges presented by greater freedom?
    - To what extent was freedom based on class and wealth?
    - Consider changes in various aspects of equality (e.g., social, economic)
    - How does affirmative action fit into the equality question?
    - How did recent immigration affect identity? How was the face of America changed? How were communities and families affected?

13. .... LO 1-5 ....FP 12 .... Text, all pages; video segments 1-5
    - Consider the gaps between the rich and the poor.
    - How and why were immigration issues similar/different?
    - How and why was the consumer culture similar/different?
    - How and why were American identity, freedom, and equality similar/different?

ENRICHMENT IDEAS

These activities are not required unless your instructor assigns them. They are offered as suggestions to help you learn more about the material presented in this lesson.

1. In a well-developed essay, compare and contrast income distribution among the American people in the periods 1880-1900 and 1980-2000. What explains the similarities and differences? (Cite your sources.)

2. Investigate current immigration policy and the major issues surrounding contemporary immigration to the United States. Then submit a report on your findings. What are your recommendations for future American policies? (Cite your sources.)

3. Research the effects of the Welfare Reform Act of 1996. What forms of assistance are currently available to the poor in America? What could be done to improve the welfare system in the United States? (Cite your sources.)

4. Investigate the issue of violence in America compared to other "developed" countries in the world. In a well-developed report, submit your findings. What explains the difference between the United States and other countries? (Cite your sources.)

5. Read the "Documenting the American Promise" feature on "Protecting Gay and Lesbian Rights" on pages 1130–1131 of the text. In a thoughtful essay, answer the questions posed in the text and provide your analysis of the status of gay and lesbian rights in the early twenty-first century.

SUGGESTED READINGS/RESOURCES

See the "Bibliography" on pages 1136–1137 and 1176–1177 of the text if you wish to examine other books and resources related to the material discussed in this lesson.

Lesson 24

A Different World

OVERVIEW

While Americans were adjusting to new political, economic, and social realities at home in the last quarter of the twentieth century, remarkable changes were occurring in the world arena. With the Cold War ending, the world became a different place. Why had this happened? What did it mean?

When President Jimmy Carter took office in 1977, the Cold War was still dominating American foreign policy. That made it difficult for Carter to apply his emphasis on human rights consistently. His diplomatic successes were overwhelmed by the Soviet Union's invasion of Afghanistan and the hostage crisis in Iran. Both episodes made the United States appear weak, and voter frustrations with that image contributed to President Carter's defeat in the 1980 presidential election.

The Cold War heated up when President Ronald Reagan referred to the Soviet Union as the real "evil empire" and escalated the arms race to the point that real "star wars" seemed a possibility. American interventions around the globe were still viewed through the prism of the worldwide communist threat. Meanwhile, Mikhail Gorbachev came to power in the Soviet Union, and the course of world history quickly changed. By the end of the 1980s, the collapse of the Berlin Wall symbolized the end of Soviet domination of Eastern Europe. The Soviet Union itself disintegrated shortly after, and the Cold War was over. What in the world was going on here?

The end of the Cold War was a turning point, but it was not the end of the story. In fact, the world was now more complex. Even as the Soviet Union was collapsing, the United States became involved in a war in the area of the Persian Gulf. This war was about aggression and oil. While access to oil would continue to be an American priority, what other national interests would compel the United States to intervene with its unparalleled power in the 1990s? Indeed, this world was different, but was it safer?

LESSON ASSIGNMENT

Text: Roark, et. al., *The American Promise*
- Chapter 30, "America Moves to the Right," pp. 1116–1119, 1132–1139
- Chapter 31, "The End of the Cold War and the Challenges of Globalization," pp. 1140–1143, 1147–1151, 1157–1160, 1175–1179

Video: "A Different World," from the series *Transforming America*

LEARNING OBJECTIVES

This lesson examines the end of the Cold War and American foreign policy in the different world of the 1990s. Upon completion of this lesson, you should be able to:

1. Assess the successes and failures of President Carter's foreign policy.

2. Explain the escalation of the Cold War in the early 1980s and how that affected American diplomacy in the third world.

3. Analyze the reasons for and consequences of the end of the Cold War.

4. Analyze the causes and consequences of the Gulf War of 1991.

5. Explain American foreign policy during the 1990s.

6. Assess how developments in this era transformed the relationship of the United States with the rest of the world.

LESSON FOCUS POINTS

The following questions are designed to help you get the most benefit from the sources selected for this lesson. For reference purposes, the video is divided into five segments: (1) Introduction, (2) "The Cold War Heats Up," (3) "The End of the Soviet Union," (4) "The New World Order," and (5) Summary Analysis: "After the Cold War."

1. Why did President Carter make human rights the cornerstone of his foreign policy? Why and how was a human rights policy difficult to administer consistently? (text, pp. 1116–1117)

2. What successes did President Carter have in foreign affairs? Why did relations with the Soviet Union become more strained toward the end of his tenure in office? (text, pp. 1117–1118)

3. Why did Iranian militants hold Americans hostage in Iran in 1979-1980? How was this crisis perceived in America? How and why did it hurt Carter's chances for reelection in 1980? (text, pp. 1117–1119; video segment 1)

4. How and why did President Reagan escalate the Cold War and the arms race with the Soviet Union in the early 1980s? What were the effects of this militarization? (text, pp. 1132–1133; video segment 2)

5. What characterized American intervention in the Middle East, Africa, and Latin America during the Reagan administrations? Why did the United States aid rebel forces in Afghanistan? Who were these people? (text, p. 1133; video segment 2)

6. What factors explain the Iran-Contra Affair? Why and how did this scandal involve serious misconduct by the Reagan administration? (text, pp. 1133–1134; video segment 2)

7. How and why did Mikhail Gorbachev initiate major changes in Soviet policies in the mid-1980s? Why and how did President Reagan and his administration respond to these initiatives? (text, pp. 1134–1136; video segment 3)

8. Why did communist governments collapse in Eastern Europe in 1989-1990? Why was the demolition of the Berlin Wall important? (text, pp. 1141–1142, 1149–1151; video segment 3)

9. Why did the Soviet Union dissolve? Why had the Cold War ended? What had been the costs and benefits of the Cold War? (text, pp. 1150–1151; video segment 3)

10. Why and how did President George H. W. Bush and his administration counter Iraq's invasion of Kuwait in 1990-1991? What were the results of the Persian Gulf War? (text, pp. 1147–1149; video segment 4)

11. Why did the Clinton administration authorize American intervention in Haiti and Kosovo? What explains the decision not to intervene in Rwanda? (text, pp. 1157–1159; video segment 4)

12. What success did President Clinton have in his attempts to broker peace in the Middle East? Why was the Palestinian-Israeli conflict so difficult? Why did the Middle East remain an area of concern for the United States? (text, pp. 1159–1160; video segment 4)

13. In summary, how and why was the relationship of the United States with the rest of the world transformed between 1977–2000? What challenges existed for the United States at the beginning of the twenty-first century? (text, all pages; video segments 1-5)

HISTORICAL EXPERTS INTERVIEWED

James Baker III, U.S. Secretary of State, 1989-1992; U.S. Secretary of Treasury, 1985-1988; Senior Partner, Baker and Botts, Houston, TX
Fraser Harbutt, Associate Professor of History, Emory University,
Joseph Nye, University Distinguished Service Professor, Kennedy School of Government, Harvard University, Cambridge, MA
John Stoessinger, Distinguished Professor of International Affairs, University of San Diego, San Diego, CA
Marilyn Young, Professor of History, New York University, New York, NY

FEATURED FAMILY MEMBERS INTERVIEWED

Edward Archuleta, Santa Fe, NM
Bill Cecil, Jr., Asheville, NC
Dianne Swann-Wright, Lake Monticello, VA

PRACTICE TEST

The following items will help you evaluate your understanding of this lesson. Use the Answer Key at the end of the lesson to check your answers or to locate material related to each question.

Multiple Choice: Choose the letter of the best answer.

1. When President Carter took office in 1977, he promised to _____.
   A. end the policy of détente spearheaded by President Nixon
   B. apply moral principles to foreign policy
   C. avoid using economic pressure or sanctions against other nations
   D. cut taxes and raise the minimum wage

2. All of the following were reasons the Iranian government was hostile to the United States after the shah left the country EXCEPT _____.
   A. the CIA's role in helping to overthrow the Mossadegh government
   B. America's close ties with Iraq
   C. longtime U.S. support for the shah
   D. the belief that the United States had undermined the religious foundations of Iran

3. All of the following were associated with the increase in military spending during the Reagan administration EXCEPT _____.
   A. pressure on the Soviet Union
   B. waste at the Pentagon
   C. growth in the federal deficit
   D. installation of a laser defense shield

4. The Iran-Contra scandal involved all of the following actions on the part of the Reagan administration EXCEPT _____.
   A. violating U.S. neutrality in the war between Iran and Iraq by selling arms to Iran
   B. channeling funds to the Contras in Nicaragua
   C. pressuring the Iranians to negotiate with Muslim terrorists
   D. illegally declaring war on Iran

5. The changes that took place in the Soviet Union in the late 1980s were primarily attributable to _____.
   A. clever diplomacy by Ronald Reagan
   B. reform proposals initiated by Mikhail Gorbachev
   C. American threats of "star wars"
   D. Russian fears of attacks from NATO forces

6. The destruction of the Berlin Wall was significant because it _____.
   A. meant the Soviet Union had lost all military power
   B. allowed West Berliners to leave Germany
   C. represented successful application of "smart" bombs
   D. symbolized the end of Soviet repression in the area

7. The United States intervened in the Iraqi invasion of Kuwait because the _____.
   A. U.S. government wanted to help the Kuwaitis spread democracy
   B. United States needed to maintain access to Kuwait's oil resources
   C. Saudi Arabian government asked the United States to send troops to Kuwait
   D. United Nations asked the United States to send troops to Kuwait

8. One consequence of America's policy in the early 1990s to stay out of foreign disputes unless its vital interests were at stake was the _____.
   A. ouster of Slobodan Milosevic from power in Serbia
   B. establishment of military rule in Haiti
   C. massacre of half a million people in a brutal civil war in Rwanda
   D. end of apartheid in South Africa

9. All of the following were consequences of the end of the Cold War EXCEPT _____.
   A. capitalism spread further in the world
   B. fear of nuclear conflagration lessened
   C. non-state groups had more freedom to operate
   D. regional alliances were no longer relevant

Short Answer: Your answer should specifically address the points indicated in one or two paragraphs.

10. Why was the Iran-Contra Affair considered "the most serious case of executive branch misconduct since Watergate?"

11. Why did the Soviet Union dissolve by 1991? Why was the dissolution important?

12. What were the standards for U.S. military intervention during the 1990s? Why were these standards applied unevenly?

Essay Question: Your response should be several paragraphs long and should elaborate on the points indicated in a manner that expresses understanding of the material.

13. How and why was the relationship of the United States with the rest of the world transformed between 1977–2000? What challenges existed for the United States at the beginning of the twenty-first century?

ANSWER KEY

	Answer	Learning Objectives	Focus Points	References
1.	B	LO 1	FP 1	Text, pp. 1116–1117
2.	B	LO 1	FP 3	Text, pp. 1117–1119; video segment 1
3.	D	LO 2	FP 4	Text, pp. 1132–1133; video segment 2
4.	D	LO 2	FP 6	Text, pp. 1133–1134; video segment 2
5.	B	LO 3	FP 7	Text, pp. 1134–1135; video segment 3
6.	D	LO 3	FP 8	Text, pp. 1149–1150; video segment 3
7.	B	LO 4	FP 10	Text, pp. 1147–1149; video segment 4
8.	C	LO 5	FP 11	Text, pp. 1157–1159; video segment 4
9.	D	LO 6	FP 13	Video segment 5

10. .... LO 2 .... FP 6 .... Text, pp. 1133–1134; video segment 2
 - Consider the seriousness of the issues involved.
 - Why would high-level officials sell arms to terrorists? Where did the money go?
 - What constitutional issues were at stake? How was the president involved?

11. .... LO 3 .... FP 9 .... Text, pp. 1150–1151; video segment 3
 - How did Mikhail Gorbachev bring about change within the Soviet Union?
 - Consider the effects of the long-standing American containment policy.
 - How did this change the world?

12. .... LO 5 .... FP 11 .... Text, pp. 1157–1159; video segment 4
 - What were the vital strategic and economic interests of the United States?
 - What role did humanitarian interests play?
 - Why did the United States avoid intervention in Rwanda?

13. .... LO 6 .... FP 13 .... Text, all pages; video segment 1–5
 - Consider how the Cold War continued to dominate policy decisions until 1991.
 - Why did the U.S. relationship with many Middle Eastern nations become tense?
 - Why did the Cold War end? What was important about that?
 - What did the Gulf War of 1991 indicate about U.S. intervention?
 - What were the standards for U.S. military intervention in the 1990s? How was this illustrated?
 - What was the position of the United States relative to the world in 2000? How was this different from 1977?
 - How could the United States be considered a threat? Who threatened the United States?

ENRICHMENT IDEAS

These activities are not required unless your instructor assigns them. They are offered as suggestions to help you learn more about the material presented in this lesson.

1. Research the genocide that took place in Rwanda in 1994 and then watch the film, *Hotel Rwanda*. In a well-developed essay, explain what happened there and why there was no intervention to stop the killing. Include in your essay an evaluation of how well the film told the story of the tragedy.

2. In a well-developed essay, compare and contrast the Persian Gulf War of 1991 with the Iraqi War that began in 2003. Include in your essay your analysis of the costs and benefits of U.S. involvement in each case.

SUGGESTED READINGS/RESOURCES

See the "Bibliography" on pages 1136–1137 and 1176–1177 of the text if you wish to examine other books and resources related to the material discussed in this lesson.

Lesson 25

Globalizing America

OVERVIEW

As the twenty-first century opened, the United States remained at the summit of the world. Its economic power stretched to the far reaches of the planet, and its military power was unmatched. In addition, the United States possessed "soft power," based on its avowed commitment to freedom, democratic values, and human rights. While these strengths made America the envy of much of the world, the nation still faced serious challenges both at home and abroad.

It was becoming clear by the early twenty-first century that the scope and intensity of this phase of economic globalization brought new problems along with opportunities. Some questioned whether "free trade" was "fair trade." Others decried the poor working conditions and environmental damage spreading throughout the world. American material culture appeared everywhere, but some felt threatened by it. The global economy was here to stay, but what were its costs and benefits?

In the midst of this rapidly changing world, global terrorism came to America on September 11, 2001. The events of that day marked a turning point for America and may have been the defining moment for the George W. Bush presidency. The American people were outraged by the attacks and briefly experienced a sense of community perhaps not felt since World War II. The president had an opportunity to lead the nation to a new level of greatness. Would he be able to meet the challenge?

In the years after the attacks, President Bush and his administration faced mounting criticism. The "war on terrorism" was costly and had no end in sight. National security was still at risk, even though Americans had given up some of their liberty. In addition, much of the world community, initially quite supportive of the United States after 9/11, expressed displeasure with the American application of preventive war in Iraq and the arrogance of American leadership. President Bush won reelection in 2004, but the national and international debates continued. What was happening here? What did it mean?

LESSON ASSIGNMENT

Text: Roark, et. al., *The American Promise*
- Chapter 31, "The End of the Cold War and the Challenges of Globalization," pp. 1140–1143, 1160–1167, 1171–1177

Video: "Globalizing America," from the series *Transforming America*

LEARNING OBJECTIVES

This lesson examines how the many dimensions of globalization continue to transform America and the world. Upon completion of this lesson, you should be able to:

1. Explain the causes and consequences of contemporary globalization.

2. Analyze the terrorist attacks on the United States on September 11, 2001, and the domestic response to those attacks.

3. Analyze the foreign policy decisions and actions of the George W. Bush administration, including the "war on terrorism" and the Iraq War.

4. Assess the transformation of America's relationships with the world and the challenges facing the nation in the world arena in the early twenty-first century.

LESSON FOCUS POINTS

The following questions are designed to help you get the most benefit from the sources selected for this lesson. For reference purposes, the video is divided into five segments: (1) Introduction, (2) "New Opportunity, New Vulnerability," (3) "9/11," (4) "The War on Terror," and (5) Summary Analysis: "The Greatest Risk."

1. What does "globalization" mean? How is the globalization of the early twenty-first century different from that of earlier eras? (text, pp. 1140–1143, 1160–1161; video segments 1, 2)

2. Why and how were the Internet and World Wide Web developed? How did they facilitate globalization? What points do critics of the Internet make? (text, pp. 1162–1163)

3. What does "free trade" mean? What arrangements did the United States enter into in order to ease trade restrictions? Who benefited and who lost as a result of these trade agreements? (text, pp. 1160–1161, 1164–1167; video segment 2)

4. Why were workers' rights and environmental issues of particular concern as economic globalization proceeded? How were these issues addressed? How could they be addressed? (text, pp. 1160–1161, 1164–1167; video segment 2)

5. How and why was the world being "Americanized" in the early twenty-first century? What effect did this have on national identity and interests? Why were some threatened by the expanding presence of America in the world? (text, pp. 1160–1161, 1164–1167; video segment 2)

6. How were the terrorist attacks on the United States on September 11, 2001, related to globalization? Why did the terrorists associated with Al Qaeda attack America? (text, pp. 1171–1172; video segments 3, 4)

7. How did the American people react to the attacks? Do you think the responses cited in the video were typical? How did you respond? (video segment 3)

8. In response to the terrorist attacks, what steps did the Bush administration and Congress take to enhance security at home? Why was the USA PATRIOT (Uniting and Strengthening America by Providing Appropriate Tools Required to Intercept and Obstruct Terrorism) Act controversial? (text, p. 1172; video segment 3)

9. What is terrorism? Why is it used? Who uses it? Why will a "war on terrorism" likely go on forever? (video segment 4)

10. How did the Bush administration approach the removal of the Taliban in Afghanistan? Why was this operation undertaken? What were the results? (text, p. 1172; video segment 4)

11. Why and how did the Bush administration move toward unilateralism before 9/11? How and why did the war on terrorism provide a rationale for a profound shift in U.S. defense policy? What elements comprised the new national defense strategy announced by President Bush? (text, pp. 1172–1173; video segment 4)

12. Why did the Bush administration decide to go to war with Iraq? What is the difference between a "preemptive" and a "preventive" war? (text, p. 1173; video segment 4)

13. Why were most of America's great-power allies and many critics at home distressed by the U.S. invasion of Iraq? (text, pp. 1173–1175; video segment 4)

14. What were the costs and benefits of the Iraq War? (text, pp. 1173–1176; video segment 4)

15. In summary, how and why had America and its place in the world been transformed by the major developments of the early twenty-first century? What major challenges lay ahead? (text, all pages; video segments 1–5)

HISTORICAL EXPERTS INTERVIEWED

Michael Bernstein, Professor of History, University of California, San Diego, CA
Karl Brooks, Assistant Professor of History, University of Kansas, Lawrence, KS
Steve Cobb, Chairperson of Department of Economics, University of North Texas, Denton, TX
Nick Gillespie, Editor-in-Chief, *Reason Magazine*, Oxford, OH
Susan Hartmann, Professor of History, Ohio State University, Columbus, OH
Joan Hoff, Research Professor of History, Montana State University, Bozeman, MT
Akira Iriye, Professor of History, Harvard University, Cambridge, MA
Joseph Nye, University Distinguished Service Professor, Kennedy School of Government, Harvard University, Cambridge, MA
John Stoessinger, Distinguished Professor of International Affairs, University of San Diego, San Diego, CA
Marilyn Young, Professor of History, New York University, New York, NY

FEATURED FAMILY MEMBERS INTERVIEWED

Edward Archuleta, Santa Fe, NM
Bill Cecil, Jr., Asheville, NC
Philip Deloria, Ann Arbor, MI
Charlene McAden, Blooming Grove, TX
Mark Neebe, Cambridge, MA
Dianne Swann-Wright, Lake Monticello, VA

PRACTICE TEST

The following items will help you evaluate your understanding of this lesson. Use the Answer Key at the end of the lesson to check your answers or to locate material related to each question.

Multiple Choice: Choose the letter of the best answer.

1. Globalization at the end of the twentieth century was _____.
   A. facilitated by new communications technology
   B. more a political process than an economic one
   C. seen as a way to limit the impact of economic disaster
   D. based on the establishment of an organization committed to world peace

2. One of the objectives of "free trade" is to _____.
   A. improve labor standards
   B. maximize consumption
   C. protect the environment
   D. increase government revenues

3. Protesters at the November 1999 demonstrations in Seattle reflected a new alliance between environmentalists and _____.
   A. big business
   B. the oil industry
   C. feminists
   D. labor unions

4. Al Qaeda's attacks on the United States on September 11, 2001, were motivated in part by the terrorists wanting to _____.
   A. initiate an era of democracy and religious tolerance in the Middle East
   B. rid the Middle East of Western influences
   C. trick the United States into launching an attack on Iraq
   D. punish the United States for its support of the Soviet Union in Afghanistan

5. At the core of the controversy over the USA PATRIOT Act was the _____.
   A. trade-off between security and liberty
   B. inadequacy of funding levels
   C. issue of compensating victims of terrorism
   D. authorization for a war against Iraq

6. The national defense strategy adopted by President George W. Bush in 2002 _____.
   A. stressed war as a last resort in settling disputes
   B. argued for preemptive use of American military power
   C. emphasized the importance of multilateralism
   D. included tax increases to fund military operations

7. All of the following can be considered major costs of the U.S.-led war in Iraq EXCEPT _____.
   A. damage to America's credibility and image in the world
   B. a substantial increase in the U.S. budget deficit
   C. diversion from the efforts to stabilize Afghanistan and destroy Al Qaeda
   D. serious damage to the political alliance between the United States and Britain

8. A problem facing the United States in its relations with the world in the early twenty-first century concerns _____.
   A. its failure to have enough nuclear weapons
   B. losing the American sense of humility
   C. squandering America's "soft power"
   D. depending too much on multilateralism

Short Answer: Your answer should specifically address the points indicated in one or two paragraphs.

9. What are the major criticisms of the free trade agreements entered into by the United States?

10. Why did Al Qaeda terrorists attack America on September 11, 2001?

11. Why did the United States go to war against Iraq in 2003? How did the rationale for the war change? What were the initial consequences of this war?

Essay Question: Your response should be several paragraphs long and elaborate on the points indicated in a manner that expresses understanding of the material.

12. How and why had America and its place in the world been transformed by the major developments of the early twenty-first century? What major challenges lay ahead for the United States in its relations with other countries?

ANSWER KEY

	Answer	Learning Objectives	Focus Points	References
1.	A	LO 1	FP 1	Text, pp. 1140–1143, 1160–1161; video segments 1, 2
2.	B	LO 1	FP 3	Text, pp. 1160–1161; video segment 2
3.	D	LO 1	FP 4	Text, p. 1161; video segment 2
4.	B	LO 2	FP 6	Text, pp. 1171–1172; video segments 3, 4
5.	A	LO 2	FP 8	Text, p. 1172; video segment 3
6.	B	LO 3	FP 11	Text, pp. 1172–1173; video segment 4
7.	D	LO 3	FP 14	Text, pp. 1173–1176; video segment 4
8.	C	LO 4	FP 15	Video segment 5

9. .... LO 1 .... FP 3 .... Text, pp. 1164–1167; video segment 2
   - Consider the effects on factory jobs in the United States.
   - How are workers treated in foreign countries?
   - What environmental issues are at stake?

10. .... LO 2 .... FP 6 .... Text, pp. 1171–1172; video segment 3, 4
    - How were these attacks connected to the global influence of America?
    - What did Osama Bin Laden (and the 9/11 Commission Report) indicate about the reasons for the attacks?

11. .... LO 3 .... FP 12–14 .... Text, pp. 1173–1176; video segment 4
    - What rationale did the Bush administration give for going to war?
    - How did the argument for war change after it began?
    - What effects did the war have at home and abroad?

12. .... LO 4 .... FP 15 .... Text, all pages; video segments 1–5
    - Consider the economic and cultural effects of globalization.
    - What was the world's reaction to the attacks of 9/11?
    - How was America affected at home by the attacks?
    - How did the United States change its national defense strategy?
    - Why was the Iraq War controversial?
    - What were the initial consequences of the Iraq War?
    - What are the major issues to be dealt with? How should the United States deal with them? Where should the United States go from here?

ENRICHMENT IDEAS

These activities are not required unless your instructor assigns them. They are offered as suggestions to help you learn more about the material presented in this lesson.

1. Research the use of terrorism in the United States during the last thirty years. Then submit a well-developed essay in which you analyze who uses terrorism, why it is used, and the consequences of its use.

2. Research the responses to the USA PATRIOT Act in your local area. Then submit a report on your findings. Include an analysis of the most controversial parts of this legislation and state your reasoned opinion on the merits of the law.

SUGGESTED READINGS/RESOURCES

See the "Bibliography" on pages 1176–1177 of the text if you wish to examine other books and resources related to the material discussed in this lesson.

Lesson 26

A More Perfect Union

OVERVIEW

History teaches everything, even the future.
—Alphonse de Lamartine

The citation above reminds us of how broad our study of the American past has been in this course and suggests that our history will affect our future. We have examined how and why the American people transformed the United States from a rural to an urban nation, from a minor role player on the world stage to the major performer. In between, we have analyzed continuity and change in our economic, social, and political history. As we go forward, we will be well served if we use the insight gained from studying the past to guide our decisions in the present and the future.

In this lesson, we will hear from our recurring experts as they help us assess the status of American equality, freedom, and identity in the early twenty-first century. As you listen, reflect on how the meaning of these themes of American history has changed over time. Given our history, the core values of America and what it stands for will continue to be contested territory in the future.

In addition, members of our recurring featured families will give us their perspectives on how their diverse personal histories represent America. This reinforces the fact that America is shaped and transformed by people like us. We all have our own story. By connecting our past with the experiences of others and those of previous generations, perhaps we can maximize future opportunities as we create our own history.

The third segment of the video allows us to think along with three visionaries who have been actively engaged in making America and the world a better place. How can our democracy be improved? How can the economy and the environment both thrive? How can our posterity live in a safer world?

Our final reflection in this lesson grows out of comments from some of the outstanding historians who have enriched this course. Listen carefully. History has always mattered. It is based on choices. Honor what's best in our past. Pursue the truth relentlessly. Help transform America and make it "a more perfect union."

LESSON ASSIGNMENT

Text: There is no text reading assignment for this lesson.

Video: "A More Perfect Union," from the series *Transforming America*

LEARNING OBJECTIVES

This lesson reflects upon the meaning of American history and the challenges and opportunities ahead. Upon completing this lesson, you should be able to:

1. Assess the status of American equality, freedom, and identity in the early twenty-first century.

2. Describe how American people and their families represent American history.

3. Describe significant challenges and opportunities in the future and what can be done to address them.

4. Consider what history teaches and how to apply the knowledge and skills acquired in this course to improve your life.

LESSON FOCUS POINTS

The following questions are designed to help you get the most benefit from the source selected from this lesson. For reference purposes, the titles for the video segments are: (1) Introduction, (2) "A Nation of Families," (3) "Visions for the 21st Century," and (4) Program Close: "A Source of Endless Surprise."

1. How is the state of equality in America in the early twenty-first century similar to its status in 1876? What are the main barriers to equality in America today? (video segment 1)

2. Why does tension exist between freedom and equality? Why is freedom always "up for grabs?" (video segment 1)

3. How and why does American identity change over time? What effect does diversity have on national unity or purpose? (video segment 1)

4. How do the families featured throughout this course in the videos represent American history? How do the comments of family members and their families' stories personify the challenges, opportunities, and dreams of Americans? (video segment 2)

5. Why does Dolores Huerta believe that practicing democracy is essential for Americans? How does she advise people to practice democracy? (video segment 3)

6. How does Amory Lovins address the challenges of reconciling a dynamic capitalist economy with the need for a healthy and sustainable environment? What characterizes his vision of a new industrial revolution? What does he consider "the big unfinished task of the twenty-first century? (video segment 3)

7. Why does James Blight believe that "not killing other human beings" is a priority for the twenty-first century? Why does the United States have a particular obligation in this regard? How can Americans help lessen the killing? (video segment 3)

8. What does the study of the past teach us? Why does it matter? What does it teach us about the future? How can you create history? (video segment 4)

HISTORICAL EXPERTS INTERVIEWED

Kenneth Alfers, Content Specialist for *Transforming America*, Professor of History, Mountain View College, Dallas, TX
Dr. Omar Ali, Assistant Professor of History, Towson University, Towson, MD
Gerard Baker, Superintendent, Mount Rushmore National Memorial, Keystone, SD
James Blight, Professor of International Relations, Watson Institute, Brown University, Providence, RI
Julian Bond, Chairman, NAACP Board of Directors, Washington, DC
H.W. Brands, Professor of History, University of Texas, Austin, TX
Clayborne Carson, Professor of History and Editor of Martin Luther King, Jr. Papers, Stanford University, Stanford, CA
Christopher Edley, Dean, University of California Law School, Berkeley, CA
Eric Foner, Professor of History, Columbia University, New York, NY
David Gutierrez, Professor of History, University of California, San Diego, CA
Steven Hahn, Professor of History, University of Pennsylvania, Philadelphia, PA
Fraser Harbutt, Associate Professor, Emory University, Atlanta, GA
Dolores Huerta, Founder, Dolores Huerta Foundation, Bakersfield, CA
Alice Kessler-Harris, Professor of History, Columbia University, New York, NY
Amory Lovins, CEO, Rocky Mountain Institute, Snowmass, CO
Jacqueline Jones Royster, Professor of English, Ohio State University, Columbus, OH
Bruce Schulman, Professor of History, Boston University, Boston, MA
Richard White, Professor of History, Stanford University, Stanford, CA
Judy Wu, Assistant Professor, Ohio State University, Columbus, OH

FEATURED FAMILY MEMBERS INTERVIEWED

Edward Archuleta, Santa Fe, NM
Bill Cecil, Jr., Asheville, NC
Philip Deloria, Ann Arbor, MI
Vine Deloria, Jr., Golden, CO
Harry Dingenthal, Garland, TX
Eddie Fung, Santa Cruz, CA
Charlene McAden, Blooming Grove, TX
Mark Neebe, Cambridge, MA
Dianne Swann-Wright, Lake Monticello, VA
Ellen Swann-Wright, Baltimore, MD
Sherrie Tarpley, Melissa, TX
Judy Yung, Santa Cruz, CA

PRACTICE TEST

The following items will help you evaluate your understanding of this lesson. Use the Answer Key at the end of the lesson to check your answers or locate material related to each question.

Multiple Choice: Choose the letter of the best answer.

1. In terms of equality, the situation in America in the early twenty-first century is similar to 1876 in respect to _____.
   A. economic and social inequality
   B. legal inequities
   C. unequal political rights for women
   D. lack of equal opportunities for the middle class

2. The idea of freedom is always "up for grabs" because _____.
   A. every group defines the term as it sees fit
   B. liberties are not adequately protected in the Constitution
   C. foreigners do not understand what the concept means
   D. immigration laws are not sufficiently enforced

3. Family members featured in the videos in this course _____.
   A. were generally pessimistic about America's future
   B. criticized the lack of opportunity in America
   C. represented the complexity of the American experience
   D. longed for a return to "the good old days"

4. According to Dolores Huerta, making changes in government and society requires all of the following EXCEPT _____.
   A. elite education
   B. self-effort
   C. direct action
   D. organization

5. Amory Lovins, author of *Natural Capitalism*, considers "the big unfinished task" of the twenty-first century to be _____.
   A. making people work more productively
   B. finding new sources of oil
   C. living in harmony with nature
   D. exploring the outer reaches of the galaxy

6. James Blight, co-author of *Wilson's Ghost*, believes that in the twenty-first century _____.
   A. an effective international organization for peace will be created
   B. proliferation of nuclear weapons is inevitable
   C. terrorists will dominate the Middle East
   D. not killing other human beings must be a priority

Short Answer: Your answer should specifically address the points indicated in one or two paragraphs.

7. Why is practicing democracy important in the twenty-first century? How should Americans do this?

8. How can a capitalist economy be reconciled with a healthy and sustainable environment in the twenty-first century? What will a new industrial revolution entail?

9. Why is "not killing other human beings" a moral imperative for the twenty-first century? How can Americans lessen the killing?

Essay Questions: Your response should be several paragraphs long and elaborate on the points indicated in a manner that expresses understanding of the material.

10. The idea of equality has been a core principle of the United States since its founding. How and why was America pushed to uphold this idea between 1877 and the present? What limits equality? What is the status of equality in America in the early twenty-first century?

11. How and why has the story of American freedom changed from 1877 to the present? What does freedom mean? How and why has freedom been limited? Why is the story of freedom unfinished?

12. Who is an American? What does being an American mean? What does America stand for in the world? How and why did American identity change between 1877 and the present? What have you learned about American identity?

ANSWER KEY

Answer	Learning Objectives	Focus Points	References
1. A	LO 1	FP 1	Video segment 1
2. A	LO 1	FP 2	Video segment 1
3. C	LO 2	FP 4	Video segment 2
4. A	LO 3	FP 5	Video segment 3
5. C	LO 3	FP 6	Video segment 3
6. D	LO 3	FP 7	Video segment 3
7.	LO 3	FP 5	Video segment 3

- Consider what happens when democracy is not practiced.
- How is the social good promoted in a democracy?
- How critical is self-effort, organization, and direct action?

8. ....LO 3......................FP 6.. Video segment 3
   - Consider the financial opportunities of natural capitalism.
   - Why is it imperative to work in harmony with nature?
   - What will likely result from a new industrial revolution?

9. ....LO 3......................FP 7.. Video segment 3
   - Why is the danger of mass killing greater in our times?
   - Why does America have a special role to play in lessening the killing?
   - What are some practical steps to reduce the killing?

10. ....LO 1......................FP 1 .... Video segments 1, 2, 4
    - Consider the political, social, and economic meanings of equality.
    - How does American society measure equality? What limits equality?
    - Who was excluded from equal rights and opportunities? How did they try to be included? What can be learned from these experiences?
    - Who is still excluded from equality today? What can be done to assure greater equality?

11. ....LO 1......................FP 2 .... Video segments 1, 2, 4
    - Consider the political, social, and economic dimensions of freedom.
    - Who defines freedom? What limits freedom?
    - Why is there tension between freedom and equality?
    - Who had freedom in 1877? How was this freedom expressed?
    - How and why did freedom change for minorities since 1877?
    - How and why did America become the leader of the "free" world? What does this mean?
    - How and why do you think the boundaries of freedom will change in the future?

12. ....LO 1......................FP 3 .... Video segments 1, 2, 4
    - How is an American defined in the Constitution?
    - What ideals does an American espouse?
    - Who tries to define what being an American means?
    - Who was excluded from being an American in 1877? How were they excluded?
    - How and why was the definition of an American broadened over time?
    - How and why has diversity changed American identity? What has been learned about diversity in America?
    - How and why has the meaning of America in the world changed?
    - What does all of this say about American identity?

ENRICHMENT IDEA

This activity is not required unless your instructor assigns it. It is offered as a suggestion to help you reflect upon and relate to the material presented in this lesson.

In a thoughtful essay, describe how your family history and you personally represent American history. Include in your essay a description of how you have been creating history and will do so in the future.

SUGGESTED READINGS

In addition to the books listed in the bibliographies referenced in previous lessons, the following selections are highly recommended to you:

James Blight and Robert McNamara, *Wilson's Ghost*
Eric Foner, *The Story of American Freedom*
Amory Lovins, *Natural Capitalism* and *Winning the Oil Endgame*

Unit IV: Fiction and Film

Recommended novels and films set in the final decades of the twentieth century:

📖 ***The Bonfire of the Vanities,*** by Tom Wolfe. This is a pyrotechnic satire of the roiling, corrupt, savage, ethnic melting pot that is New York City in the 1980s.

📖 ***Prayer at Rumayla,*** by Charles Sheehan-Miles. Chet Brown arrived home from Desert Storm to find that the war was only beginning. Betrayed by his friends, ignored by his family, he travels across the country in an attempt to find answers to questions he doesn't even know to ask.

📖 ***So Far from God: A Novel***, by Ana Castillo. This is an inventive novel about the fortunes of a contemporary Chicana family in the village of Tome, New Mexico. It is a tale of magical realism, both tragic and funny; a hymn to women's endurance and to the harshness of their lives.

📖 ***The Lone Ranger and Tonto Fistfight in Heaven***, by Sherman Alexie. In these tales of modern life on the Reservation, Alexie's grit, humor, and lyricism perfectly capture the absurdity of a proud people living in squalor, struggling to survive in a society they disdain.

📖 *1984*, by George Orwell. *Newspeak, doublethink, thoughtcrime*—Orwell created a whole set of words concerning totalitarian control that have since passed into our common vocabulary. Once considered futuristic, it now conjures fear because of how closely it fits our current reality.

🎬 *Angels in America,* d. Mike Nichols. This powerful film adaptation of Tony Kushner's epic play is an astonishing mix of philosophy, politics, and vibrant gay soap opera that summed up the Reagan era for an entire generation of theater-goers.

🎬 *El Norte,* d. Gregory Nava. This drama is about a Guatemalan brother and sister who flee their native land, due to ethnic and political persecution, and come to America (*El Norte*) in search of a better life.

🎬 *Do the Right Thing,* d. Spike Lee. Lee purposefully and ambiguously explores escalating racial tensions on one Bedford-Stuyvesant block on the hottest day of the summer. This is a deliberately unsettling and provocative film, but it is also brimming with exuberance and color.

🎬 *Three Kings,* d. David O. Russell. Four disillusioned U.S. soldiers decide to steal $23 million in gold hijacked from Kuwait by Saddam Hussein's army. This tale of greed and compassion is set among the dust and desolation of Iraq during the first Gulf War.

🎬 *Wag the Dog,* d. Barry Levinson. This is a nervy satire of a presidential crisis and the people who whitewash the facts. With the similarities between history and this film, *Wag* will be forever linked to the Monica Lewinsky saga.

🎬 *Hotel Rwanda,* d. Terry George. This is a true story of a hotel manager in Rwanda who in 1994 saved 1,200 "guests" during the genocidal clash between tribal Hutus, who slaughtered a million victims, and the horrified Tutsis, who found safe haven or died.